Loving the Torah More Than God?

Other Books by the Same Author

CHRIST PROCLAIMED

GROUNDED IN LOVE

CATHOLIC IDENTITY AFTER VATICAN II

GOD ENCOUNTERED:
VOLUME I: UNDERSTANDING THE CHRISTIAN FAITH

Loving the Torah More Than God?

Towards a Catholic Appreciation of Judaism

Frans Jozef van Beeck, S. J.

Foreword by Eugene B. Borowitz

A Campion Book

Loyola University Press

Chicago 60657

Acknowledgments are due to the following:

Mr. Zvi Kolitz, of New York City, for permission to reprint the first published version (1947) of his story *Yossel Rakover's Appeal to God*;

The Johns Hopkins University Press, of Baltimore, Maryland, for permission to print the author's English translation of Emmanuel Levinas' essay *Aimer la Thora plus que Dieu*;

Marc Chagall, *White Crucifixion*, oil on canvas, 1938, 154.3 x 139.7 cm., gift of Alfred S. Alschuler, © 1989 The Art Institute of Chicago. All rights reserved.

Imprimi potest:
Very Rev. Robert A. Wild, S. J., Provincial, Chicago Province
February 6, 1989

Printed and bound in the United States of America.

Library of Congress Cataloging-in-Publication Data
Beeck, Frans Jozef van.
    Loving the Torah more than God? : towards a Catholic appreciation of Judaism / Frans Jozef van Beeck.
    p. cm.
    Bibliography: p.
    Includes index.
    ISBN 0-8294-0620-4
    1. Judaism – Relations – Catholic Churce. 2. Catholic Churce – Relations – Judaism. 3. Kolitz, Zvi, 1931 - Yosl Rakovers vendung tsu Got. 4. Holocost (Jewish theology) 5. Levinas, Emmanuel – Views on Judaism. 6. Judaism (Christian theology) 7. Catholic Church – Doctrines. I. Title.
BM535.B365 1989
261.2'6 – dc 20   89-12391
                                                                              CIP

This book is for

the Roberts House Community at Boston College,

friends in the Lord,

1977-1985.

Contents

THREE: God's Love and God's Law

Foreword

This book fascinates, inspires and challenges all at once. It can be read as an entrancing excavation of the fruitful misreadings which go to make up a tradition, whether Jewish, Christian or Judeo-Christian. It is also a theological rumination which is learned and incisive, yet deeply moving. We do not often see an erudite thinker responding in openness to a searching critic of his religion by seeking to untangle the authentic from the misguided in his received doctrine. Moreover, centuries of unhappy exchanges between protagonists of Christianity and Judaism have, even in the recent history of civility, rarely produced a document such as this in which admirable self-respect is balanced by respect for others. And it breaks new ground in interfaith discussion by suggesting, in a most irenic, gentle but compelling way that it is time to move toward the most difficult question: in this case, what Jews might consider learning from Christianity.

All this arises by way of a story and a commentary on a commentary on a translation of a translation of the original! The immediate focus of the author's theological reflection is Emmanuel Levinas's radio lecture based on the French version of the Yiddish rendering of Zvi Kolitz's English tale, "Yossel Rakover's Appeal to God." Thus this intellectual feast begins with a fiction about fact, a story about a believing Jew's last statement as he awaits death from the Nazis finally ending the rebellion in the Warsaw Ghetto. The moment was rendered with such verisimilitude that the fiction came to be accepted as a historic document when submitted as such to a Yiddish journal by an Argentine Jew, its apparent translator. And, it should be noted, that it was widely accepted as such long after Kolitz called attention to its origins.

This data is important because the title of this work, *Loving the Torah More than God?* derives not merely from Levinas's title but from a theme in the Yiddish translation, one that is *not* found in Kolitz's English story. We can, I think, learn a good deal about modern Judaism, better, about the efforts to modernize Judaism, if we attend to what each of these authors has sought to convey.

Kolitz's Yossel is a Gerer Hasid, a member of one of the most observant and pietistic of contemporary Jewish groups. His words rehearse traditional Jewish beliefs about God's justice, or apparent lack of it, about human suffering and dignity, and about the character and destiny of the Jewish people. Yet Yossel is also surprisingly modern for a Hasid. He writes in a thoroughly Westernized fashion, with almost self-conscious attention to good style and apt language. Coming from a community which normally approaches these topics by *midrash* or tale, he is remarkably abstract and reflective about his beliefs. Most significantly, however, he is a political activist, a rebel who takes up arms against his people's oppressors. Should an occasional Hasid argue with God, we would not be surprised; Levi Yitzchak of Berditchev set the model for such post-Job-ian daring. But it is quite another thing to suggest that a devout pietist would forsake the quietism of his movement to take up arms, even against the Nazis. Thus today in the State of Israel, most Hasidim do not, as a matter of principle, serve in the armed forces.

Our intellectual journey, therefore, begins with Kolitz's inspiring creation, a figure in whom he integrates the profundities of classic Jewish piety and modernity's passion for dignity and self-assertion, particularly against evil. Surely a major reason why this fiction was later so widely accepted as fact is that Kolitz reflects here what many Jews would like Judaism to be—richly traditional yet fully modern.

The anonymous Yiddish translator gave Yossel a radically different point of view. After line 234 of the original, he interpolated these two striking sentences: "I love Him, but I love His Torah more, and even if I had deceived myself in His regard, I would nonetheless observe His Torah. God means religion, but His Torah means a way of life, and the more we die for such a way of life, the more immortal it becomes." Read quickly, these words simply slip into Yossel's diction. He is, after all, an observant Jew. But on reflection something very much more is at stake, indeed something that utterly transforms Kolitz's already recreated Gerer Hasid.

The anonymous translator is almost certainly a Yiddishist, and the provenance he chose for his "translation" was the great Yiddishist literary journal functioning after the Holocaust, *Die Goldene Kait, The Golden Thread.* In the spirit of Yiddishist secularity he has by his interpolation made the erstwhile pietist Yossel the spokesman of his ideology. All this goes back to the late nineteenth century when several modernizing Jewish movements took it for granted that sophisticated moderns could no longer believe in religion; it was the Jewish version of what a later generation would call the "death of

God." Unlike the Zionists who secularized into nationalism and, in due course into Hebraism, the Yiddishists believed, following the European model, that nationality could exist through language and high culture alone. Since the common Jewish language of the mass of European Jews was Yiddish and not Hebrew, they sought to make it the language of modern Jewish expression and continuity. By "Torah" they meant a Yiddishist cultural "way of life," one whose immortality is found in achievement in this world, not in any supernatural promise. A Hasid could not easily love the Torah more than God, being commanded by it, as he knew by his several daily recitations, "to love the Lord, your God, with all your heart, with all your soul, and with all your might." But a secular Yiddishist would gladly give up the old piety, which many Yiddishist writers had attacked, for a life of high humanistic Yiddish culture. Isaac Bashevis Singer remains the great exemplar of this fading possibility—and though he still writes in Yiddish, almost all Jews today read him in English.

This interpolation was, in fact, intensified in the French translation, so that it now reads "but I love his Torah *even* more." (Was this because it was to be published in a French Zionist journal? or was this French rationalism asserting itself?) Delightfully, it was precisely this intensified interpolation that caught Levinas's eye and became the pivot of his lecture. But he comes to these words not as a cultural secularist but as a deeply religious philosopher. For Levinas these sentences reflected his own modernistic reinterpretation of "Torah," one derived from his predecessors in modern Jewish rationalism, though given his unique phenomenological grouping. Essentially, he understands "Torah" and the Jewish "way of life" that it enjoins as ethics. Like Hermann Cohen, the great neo-Kantian who first gave this theme full academic exposition, God is the foundation of our moral striving, the critical effort in which we find the fulfillment of our humanhood. He can, then, speak of loving Torah "even more" than loving God because, in the line of neo-Kantian rationalism now become phenomenology, the ethical is more certain than the theological, and religious truth logically builds from its base.

Levinas also takes up and continues in his own telling fashion the neo-Kantian Jewish polemic against Christianity. Its teaching is insufficiently ethical, a failing that arises from the nature of its belief, which is blind to the centrality of the good deed. After the Holocaust and what Jews perceive to be the gross display of all the old inadequacies of Christianity in their non-response to it, the old attack comes with a telling bite. And let me add, that though most Jews today do not share, even in some popularized fashion, the neo-Kantian or phenomenological framework that gives rise to this committed Jewish ethicism, they largely agree with its basic thrust. Judaism, they will say, is essentially ethical action, and that makes it superior to Christianity which centers on gaining and exemplifying a saving faith. So Levinas had little difficulty in picking up the Yiddishist call to make high culture primary and reading into it his own message, that the (Jewish) ethical act is more significant than (Christian) faith in God.

And now to this steady procession of misreadings which Jewish tradition calls the "chain of tradition," I have taken the liberty of adding my own. In exempting the author of this work from the list, I mean to compliment him for the high academic and human standard of his own reading of these documents. Exercising exemplary discipline he is as careful as one can be to try to read what he sees before him, indeed carefully comparing versions and texts so that redaction criticism will help him clarify just what it is that he is commenting about. In the long ugly history of interfaith exchange, we have not often seen such a meticulous effort to understand "the other," his heart as well as his mind. Of course, it is one of the author's primary points that for a believing Christian, Jews ought not be simple religious "others" but part of the family of one's faith, though not in its immediate core.

This careful reading has led the author back to his own belief to see if there is substance to Levinas's charges, whose ethical standards of judgment he accepts as applicable to Christianity. His measured, sensitive evaluation of where some of its historic developments have not been true to its sublime truth and his careful, deeply felt exposition of what he understands that truth to be as it applies here, made me not only a deeply respectful but also an admiring reader. None of us finds it easy in the face of cogent criticism to obey the moral imperative to transcend defensiveness and learn what we can. It is a particularly precious ideal for the leaders and teachers of all religious traditions, since they properly stake their lives and eternal destiny on the truths they proclaim.

I shall look forward to seeing how other Catholic writers and Christians generally respond to the author's interpretation of Christianity. But I do not wish to conclude these remarks without calling attention to what I find to be the climax of this extraordinary work.

In his last pages, having opened his heart to Judaism's wounded cries to Christianity, having searched his soul to ascertain where the Jewish indictment might have merit, having then restated what he takes to be authentic Christianity, he most gently wonders if Jews might not be able now to do something somewhat similar, to see what they can make of Christian truth. His suggestion grows from the logic of his argument, for if, as his Christian faith affirms, Jesus is a fulfillment of classic Jewish faith (though not thereby an invalidation of it), might there not be something Jews could learn from Christianity about their own belief? These soft sentences say a lot about the relationship between believing Jews and Christians that the author now hopes is possible. Beyond treating each other with dignity and acknowledging all we have in common, beyond being able to discuss civilly our past hurts and present differences, the author is ready to move on to the level of mutual challenge. He accepts that of Judaism and responds to it with nobility—and then in all self-respect and in equal respect for the maturity of Jewish thinkers, he quietly inquires if they might be ready to do the same.

I welcome his loving queries, though this is not the place to respond to them. They reminded me of an address I gave in Chicago, the city of Loyola University, to the 1966 convention of the Religious Education Association. Though that body had for years been one of the few places where Catholics, Protestants and Jews met together to discuss matters of mutual interest, this assembly had a special air of excitement about it. The Protestant community was heady with talk of ecumenism. The Catholics were present in unprecedented numbers and good will under the impact of Vatican II. And we perennial outsiders, the Jews, were astounded at the prospects for a new openness and mutuality among the faiths of the American religious community. I was invited to speak as part of a three-faith plenary session on the general theme of ecumenical spirit. What I said was that we should not truly exemplify it until we had gone beyond good will and deeper understanding to the point where we could argue our differences with love, in what I then called I-thou polemics. It has been a long wait to see if that hope could be fulfilled on either side. In this book, it has.

Eugene B. Borowitz

Sigmund L. Falk Distinguished Professor of Education
and Jewish Religious Thought
Hebrew Union College—Jewish Institute of Religion
The New York School

xiii

Preface

The matters contained in this book were first presented at Loyola University of Chicago in the late Fall of 1988 in the form of the Fourth Annual John Cardinal Cody Lectures. The original presentation used some of the attractive possibilities available to live communication. Thus there were dramatic readings, by persons other than the lecturer, of the two lengthy texts by modern Jewish authors featured in the first two sections of this book; these readings were preceded by introductory remarks and followed by interpretative comments. At one point in the first lecture, a reproduction of Marc Chagall's *White Crucifixion* appeared on a large screen.

Not surprisingly, preparing the lectures for publication in book form required rearrangements of the materials presented in the lectures, to suit the solitary reader's situation, which is so different from that of the live audience. At the same time, however, there seemed to be merit in trying to preserve at least some of the liveliness and directness of the original occasion. Hence, I decided to keep the oral-acoustical tone of the lectures largely intact, rather than entirely rewriting them in expository prose to accommodate the silent reader. This decision accounts, among other things, for the continued frequent use of the first person singular.

The first lecture contained passages of a rather more personal nature. The reader will notice that one of them still occurs in the Introduction. Of the passages omitted in the present text, the most significant was the dedication of the lectures to the memory of my first violin teacher, the late Samuel Schuyer. I wish to repeat it here. Samuel Schuyer was born in The Hague, on September 9, 1873, into a family of musicians. He received his training in violin, bassoon, and theory at the Royal Conservatory in his native city. After an early career that involved positions as principal bassoonist in a variety of places as well as a European tour as a bassoon soloist, he became first assistant concertmaster at the French Opera in The Hague, and subsequently concertmaster at the Opera of Ghent, in Belgium. After a short stay in Paris, he returned to The Hague, where he became very active as a violinist and teacher, and occasionally also as a composer. He was sixty-nine years old when, in late November, 1942, he was taken from his apartment and transported to the transit camp at Westerbork. On December 8, 1942, he was put on the train to Auschwitz, where he was killed on the day of his arrival, December 11, 1942. May he live in peace.

The 1988 Cody lectures took about three months to prepare. In reality, however, they had been in the making for a much longer time—ever since 1969, when I first read Emmanuel Levinas' intriguing radio broadcast *Aimer la Thora plus que Dieu* in a Dutch translation. My deep interest in this piece (to which the title of this book continues to bear witness) turned into a resolve to pursue the matter to the end. Amid the pressures of other projects, I continued to work on it intermittently over a period of almost twenty years.

In the course of those years, I experienced the kindness of many people, many of them Jews who helped me pick my way through an unfamiliar world. Let me simply mention all those who helped me, Jews and Christians, in the order in which, as I recall, their friendly services occurred: Rev. Dries van den Akker, S.J., Barry Walfish, Dr. Arye Motzkin, Rev. Joseph D. Gauthier, S.J., Rabbi Morris Fishman, Dr. Anita Abraham, Rabbi Dr. David Novak, Dr. Paul Davidovits (whose delicate yet firm encouragement I shall always remember), Dr. Jeffrey Mallow (professor of physics at Loyola University of Chicago, who started out by putting me through my Yiddish paces and ended up by becoming a most devoted supporter of the project), Mrs. Esther M. Caplan, and Rev. Thomas H. Tobin, S.J. For information on the late Samuel Schuyer I am indebted to Mr. F. W. Zwart, Conservator of the Music Department of the Dutch Music Archives in the Gemeentemuseum in The Hague, and to Mrs. P. C. Gerritse, of the staff of the Rijksinstituut voor Oorlogsdocumentatie in Amsterdam. I also owe so many thanks to my fellow-Jesuit Matthew E. Creighton, who offered to read the page-proofs, and to my graduate assistant José Pedrozo, who was kind enough to put together the indices.

One more name, a crucial one, must be mentioned with much respect and gratitude in this context. In the course of an extensive personal correspondence, Mr. Zvi Kolitz, the author of *Yossel Rakover's Appeal to God*, came to take a very personal interest in the final stages of the preparation of the lectures. He also graciously gave me permission to reproduce the full text of his story in the published version.

Finally, three friends and colleagues at Loyola University of Chicago deserve to be especially remembered in this book. Dr. John S. Shea, of the Department of English, and Dr. Ardis B. Collins, of the Department of Philosophy, readily agreed to contribute their literary, philosophical, and especially their dramatic talents to the lectures. Without them, the audience would have had only myself to listen to, much to their loss. And unforgettably, Dr. Jon Nilson, of the Department of Theology, took care of all the details connected with the lecture series while I was temporarily overseas, with the kind of devotion that can come only from unfeigned friendship.

Loyola University of Chicago
Epiphany Sunday, January 8, 1989

Frans Jozef van Beeck, S. J.

Introduction:
Separateness and Asymmetry

Judaism and Christianity

Quite a few moments of doubt and irresolution came to me in the wake of the decision to treat the materials contained in this book. Even though the Scriptures of Israel—the *Tenakh*: the Law, the Prophets, and the Writings—are very much part of the world I inhabit, the plain fact remains that I am in no way an expert on Judaism. And let it be added at once, in preparing the materials I realized at the earliest possible stage that a few months of hard work were not going to change that situation. Consequently, I have not even tried.

Not only am I no expert on Judaism; I also decided not to refer to the many important modern attempts to clarify the relationship between Judaism and Christianity. Thus—to mention what I think is one of the most fruitful instances of Jewish-Christian dialogue in this century—the debate between Franz Rosenzweig and Eugen Rosenstock-Huessy has been left untouched, nor, for another example, have I treated the stimulating writings published by Pinchas Lapide in recent years.

The reasons for this decision are not far to seek. The relatively narrow compass of the lectures out of which this book grew made a review of the sprawling, and rather disparate, literature prohibitive. In addition, my decision to concentrate on the interpretation of two modern Jewish texts left little room for a survey of other, more directly theological treatments.

Finally, there was from the start a specifically Jesuit agenda behind this project. In the course of a twenty-year teaching career at two Jesuit Universities in the United States, I have had the privilege of experiencing the friendship as well as the competence of many

Jewish colleagues. I have also seen the generosity of many Jewish benefactors toward the Jesuit effort in higher education, and I have come to understand some of its motivations. In general, Jesuit and other Catholic universities in the United States have not been remiss in recognizing these significant Jewish contributions, but—unless my observations deceive me—the recognition has been of a humane and social nature rather than of an intellectual and theological one. Several Jewish friends and colleagues have asked me, over the years, why we seemed so reluctant to take them on intellectually. To the extent that there is truth in this last observation, the present book represents a modest attempt at recognizing the Jewish contribution to Jesuit higher education in an intellectual and theological manner.

The result of all of this is that this book concentrates on some theological issues implicit in the relationship between Judaism and Christianity themselves rather than on the history of the relationship; and specifically, it concentrates on these issues from a professedly Catholic, and even Jesuit, perspective. Hence, I will be interpreting, explaining, and arguing, not as an expert on Judaism but as a Catholic theologian, and as one who has a *concern* to share in the area of Jewish-Christian relationships and—especially in the third section—as one who has a few *theological suggestions* to make.

The *concern* has been with me for a very long time. It can be expressed as follows. Christians, including Christian theologians, tend to be unaware of, and ignorant about, Judaism as a *separate*, independent, living religious tradition. This is not a merely personal or incidental problem, but an historic, institutional one. Ever since the first century, our religious traditions have *de facto* gone their separate ways. The separation was reinforced very early on by the large number of Gentiles who responded to the Christian mission, so that the original Jewish-Christian communities became increasingly marginal and died out at an early stage. However, the separation was no less reinforced by antagonism and controversy. Polemics promoted a growing tradition of anti-Judaism in the Christian Church; traces of it can already be found in the New Testament.[1] And since polemics tend to be mutual, polemics also fed the anti-Christian animus evident, in places, in rabbinical Judaism at an early stage. Not infrequently, pagan authorities availed themselves of the friction between Jews and Christians to play off the two against one another for their own political ends.

"Asymmetry": Three Instances

Still, there is more amiss here than a tradition of ignorance or mutual animus. And incredible though it may seem, after the horror of the Holocaust, there is more amiss here even than the need for a penitential acknowledgment of anti-Semitism as a blot on the history of Christianity.[2] What is the matter is a very problematic conviction that lies at the root of the Christian tradition. The conviction is that in the relationship between Judaism and Christianity there prevails not mutuality but a fundamental *asymmetry*. Not surprisingly, Jews have always been extremely distrustful of this conviction.

Three characteristic instances will serve to illustrate this. To start with a very early example, dating back to the beginning of the second century, the asymmetry is very clearly (as well as very bluntly) stated by Saint Ignatius of Antioch. In his letter to the Magnesians he writes:

> It is senseless to profess Jesus Christ and practice Judaism. For Christianity did not come to believe in Judaism, but Judaism in Christianity, in which every tongue that came to believe in God has been gathered together [cf. Is 66, 18].[3]

Ignatius is equivalently saying that Judaism—even universalist Judaism, whose language he is employing—is *passé*.[4] True universalism, he says, is Christian, not Jewish. The relationship between the two religions, therefore, is lopsided: whereas Christianity fully accounts for Judaism, Judaism does not account for Christianity. What, therefore, once began as a *privilege* extended, in the Christian communities, to Gentile converts—namely that their new-found freedom in Christ absolved them from the prescriptions of the Mosaic law—has started to become, in the Churches dominated by converts from paganism, a Gentile *victory* over Judaism. Allow me to suggest, in passing, that modern Jews can be excused for taking offense at such statements.

Let me quote another witness—one who was writing more than a thousand years later, in A.D. 1146. Saint Bernard of Clairvaux is imploring the archbishop of Mainz to take measures against an itinerant monk whose sermons are inciting violence against Jews. Bernard's protest is obviously compassionate and sincere, but for all that, it is a shocking alternative he proposes. He writes:

> Is it not a far better triumph for the Church to convince and convert the Jews than to put them all to the sword? Has that prayer which the Church offers for the Jews [...] that the veil may be taken from their hearts so that they may be led from the darkness of error into the light of truth, been instituted in vain?[5]

Saint Bernard's words do bear witness to his condemnation of what we would now call anti-Semitism, but at a deeper level they are hardly respectful. Bernard, along with most of the Christian tradition, apparently views Jews almost exclusively as candidates for conversion to Christianity.

Even in our own more moderate days, the Christian postulate of asymmetry is far from dead. Let one characteristic example suffice to make the point. In the atmosphere of mutual tolerance and even appreciation that has happily come to characterize relations between Jews and Christians in the United States since the Second World War and the horror of the Holocaust, the phrase "Judeo-Christian tradition" has been heard with increasingly frequency. But let us face it: it is mainly *Christians* that use it, not Jews. It is wise, therefore, to be distrustful of the phrase, since it falsely suggests that Christians have a firm, reliable *religious* tradition *in common* with Judaism. It must be pointed out that Christians do *not* have such a common religious tradition.[6] Or at least they do not have it to the extent that they like to imagine they do, principally on the basis of the Scriptures which they share with Judaism; for the fact is that Christians read and interpret and live by these Scriptures in substantially different ways. It is sensible, therefore, to conclude that the Christian faith's professed dependence on Israel, combined with the lack of a reliable tradition shared by Jews and Christians, add up to a situation of considerable ambivalence—an ambivalence compounded in our day by an enduring, unsettling awareness of the mental scars left by the Holocaust.[7] All of this continues to make attempts at mutual understanding very precarious, if also very essential.

For a Catholic theologian, therefore, two attitudes must characterize the project to be undertaken in this book: a certain modesty born out of Christian ignorance about Judaism as a separate tradition, and a deep respect born out of reverence for the victims of the Holocaust that brought the people of Israel so close to the brink of extinction. Hence the subtitle of this book: *Towards a Catholic Understanding of Judaism.*

A Theological Task Animated by Personal Memories

The final intention of the argument contained in this book is *theological*: I wish to offer a reinterpretation of that ancient, fundamental Christian conviction about the asymmetry in the relationship between Jews and Christians. This reinterpretation will be offered to Christians first, but also to Jews, and not for acceptance but for examination and reflection. The third section of this book will be especially devoted to this fundamental theme of Christian theology.

Before we reinterpret, however, we must notice, appreciate, and learn. The first two sections will be devoted to this. In them, readers are invited to allow themselves to be questioned and tested by reading and interpreting two modern Jewish texts that are as beautiful as they are challenging to Christians as well as, I suspect, to Jews. The first is a short story, entitled *Yossel Rakover's Appeal to God*, by the American-Jewish author Zvi Kolitz; the second is a profoundly theological commentary on a French version of that story, by the French-Lithuanian Jewish philosopher Emmanuel Levinas, entitled *Aimer la Thora plus que Dieu*: "To Love the Torah More than God."

In treating the subject matter of this book, however, I acknowledge that I do not have only theological reasons for choosing Zvi Kolitz' story and Emmanuel Levinas' commentary. I have *personal* ones, too. When I first read these modern Jewish writings, they revived deep and lasting memories in myself, memories from the days when I was an eleven and twelve year old boy in The Hague, in The Netherlands: the embarrassing sight of the yellow stars below the left lapels of the overcoats of sad, fearful, and unspeakably distant-looking people in the streets in the early war years; the anti-Jewish slogans on billboards and the reports on anti-Jewish measures in newspapers; the swift, menacing arrests and deportations of silent, seemingly uncomplaining Jewish men, women, and children in our streets. Most painfully of all, at least for me personally, I recall the dreadful late afternoon of Wednesday, November 25, 1942, when, as a boy of twelve, a few days before my father's birthday, I walked back home in tears, having found the front door of the house of the kindly old gentleman who was my violin teacher secured by means of a seal whose significance we had come to understand only too well. His name was Samuel Schuyer. He was the first Jew I was privileged to meet and learn from, and thank God, not the last.

A few more words by way of introduction. I had been familiar with Levinas' commentary long before I found Zvi Kolitz' story. The theological reflections contained in this book, therefore, are most immediately the result of Levinas' inspiration. In fact, it was Levinas' commentary that so stimulated my theological imagination that I set out on a search for the story that had inspired Levinas. I succeeded in securing the anonymous French version that Levinas had used in 1973. By a happy coincidence—a chance conversation in the periodicals room of a theological college in that same year— this French version was identified for me as an original story written in English by Zvi Kolitz.[8] Only much later, in 1985, did I find the anonymous Yiddish version of Kolitz' story, entitled *Yosl Rakover Ret tsu G-ot*—the text that had served as the basis for the French version.[9]

ONE

Yossel Rakover's Appeal to God

Preliminaries

Zvi Kolitz' short story *Yossel Rakover's Appeal to God*, which is the subject of this first section, requires two preliminary explanations. The first deals with matters that are very much pertinent to the author's original intentions in writing the story, namely, the history which the story memorializes and against whose background it is set. The second explanation is concerned with the fact that not long after its first publication and unbeknownst to the author the story started to lead a life of its own, which led to interesting developments.

The Historical Background: The Warsaw Ghetto Uprising of April, 1943

In writing *Yossel Rakover's Appeal to God*, Zvi Kolitz was inspired by an inscription that was found after the Second World War on the wall of a cellar in the West German city of Cologne, where a number of Jews had hidden themselves for the entire duration of the war. It read: "I believe in the sun even when it is not shining, I believe in love even when feeling it not; I believe in God even when he is silent." More importantly, however, Kolitz was inspired by one particular episode of the Holocaust: the final stage of the annihilation of the Jews in Warsaw, in the spring of 1943. The history of those appalling events—a history almost too shocking to tell—must be briefly recounted.

A succession of violent measures had preceded the final annihilation. As early as November, 1940, the operation had entered upon its first stage, when the Jews were confined to the least attractive sections of the Jewish quarter, which had been sealed off by a ten-foot high wall. By the end of January, 1941, almost one hundred thousand Jews from various other quarters had been added to the original ghetto population of almost four hundred thousand. Thus, about four hundred and fifty thousand Jewish people found themselves crowded into an urban prison of less than two square miles. Ordinary rooms housed as many as twenty-five people. The only green area within the enclosure was the cemetery. There was no access to the river, and, even more importantly, no access to the economic life of the city. For a year and a half, there were no sources of income. The only thing the ghetto could do to survive was to deplete itself economically. Starvation set in, tuberculosis began to spread, and bestial ill-treatment by Nazis, especially of wealthier Jews, became the rule.

The second stage was the reign of terror, grandly announced as the "resettlement in the East" of all the "unproductive" people in the ghetto. It started on the very the day it was announced, July 22, 1942. Starving people, enticed by the irresistible promise of three loaves of bread and a two-pound jar of marmalade, allowed themselves to be picked up by the thousands at designated collection points, along with thirty pounds of personal effects, with a view to their alleged resettlement. They had, of course, been specifically instructed to take their jewelry along with them. They were loaded on to trains that left the city twice a day—as many as twelve thousand per train. The destination: Treblinka. Those offering even a semblance of resistance, those not quick enough to move, and those too young or too old to travel, were shot on the spot. In fifty dreadful days, the "great liquidation" of the Warsaw ghetto was complete: more than three hundred and ten thousand men, women, and children had been deported to the death camps or killed locally. Thousands had managed to escape and hide in the city, but by September 12, 1942, as many as seventy thousand people were still left in a ghetto that the Nazis had also gradually reduced in size.

In the face of certain death, a group of Jews inside the ghetto and some groups of Polish patriots on the outside abandoned all illusions, and formed, on December 2, 1942, the Jewish Combat Organization, which bound itself, by compact, to resist any further "resettlements" by force of arms, and to carry out terrorist actions against anyone collaborating with the Nazis. Arms were purchased in secret and distributed. Together with the Jewish Military Association, the Jewish Combat Organization succeeded in killing more than sixty informers and provocateurs inside the ghetto during the winter of 1942-3. In January of 1943, a fresh attempt at "resettlement" met with armed resistance, which led to a bloodbath among the inhabitants of the ghetto and to more deportations; it also marked the first loss of Nazi life. More arms were secretly shipped into the ghetto.

This set the scene for the final struggle. At daybreak on Monday, April 19, 1943, the fourteenth day of Nissan—that is, on the eve of

Passover, *Erev Pesach*—German troops encircled the ghetto and SS troops moved in with the support of tanks and heavy artillery. The Jewish resistance fighters had occasional help from the Polish underground outside the ghetto walls. After twenty days, on May 8, the last resistance was crushed. A week later, the commanding officer, SS General Jürgen Stroop, sent a cable to his superior to report that the former Jewish section of Warsaw no longer existed and that the synagogue had been destroyed. He put "the total number of identified and exterminated Jews" at fifty-six thousand and sixty-five.[1]

It is on the tenth day of this struggle, April 28, 1943, that Zvi Kolitz' story is set.

The History of Zvi Kolitz' Story

Zvi Kolitz published *Yossel Rakover's Appeal to God* in 1947 in a volume of "stories and parables" inspired by the Holocaust.[2] Seven years later, the editor of a Yiddish journal, the poet Avram Sutzkever, published a Yiddish translation of the story under the title *Yosl Rakover Ret tsu G-ot.*[3] It was a pirated piece of work; not only did the translator fail to identify himself, the story itself was presented as anonymous. The original epigraph about the inscription on the cellar wall in Cologne had also been left out.

Understandably, many came to think that the piece was an authentic last will and testament, retrieved from the rubble of the Warsaw ghetto. Thus, when a collection of personal testimonials to modern Jewish faith in God, entitled *I Believe*, was published in Jerusalem in 1965, it included a modern Hebrew translation of the Yiddish version, under the title *Yosl Rakover in Conversation with his Creator.* In the table of contents, the piece was simply identified as "a will."[4] From the United States, in a letter to the editor of an Israeli journal, Zvi Kolitz gently protested that the story was not historical but fictional and that he was its original author.[5]

The Yiddish translation, however, had not only dropped Kolitz' name; it had also undergone a process of revision. This is understandable. A story like Kolitz', appealing, as it does, to such a deeply neuralgic theme as the Holocaust, is likely to elicit passionate responses, and hence, it will invite commentary. That is to say, at the hands of an editor, it will invite editorializing,[6] and at the hands of a translator, it will invite expansion. Not surprisingly, therefore, the Yiddish version shows both: the anonymous translator availed himself of his freedom in order to introduce seven major expansions as well as a large number of relatively small changes.

In the text of *Yossel Rakover's Appeal to God* published in this book, the *expansions* found in the Yiddish text have been translated and inserted into the original text, but in *indented paragraphs*; the most important *changes* have been listed in footnotes and identified by means of the abbreviation *Y*. Among these changes, one stands out for sheer curiosity: Zvi Kolitz' "Yossel, son of David Rakover" has become "Yossel, son of *Yossel* Rakover"—a feature that is all the more astonishing in view of the fact that Ashkenazy Jews do not name their children after living relatives, and least of all after themselves.

The Yiddish version was in turn translated into French by Arnold Mandel; it appeared in the March 15, 1955 issue of *La Terre Retrouvée*, the Zionist newspaper published in Paris. It was this version that Emmanuel Levinas noticed, and which inspired him to write his radio broadcast *Aimer la Thora plus que Dieu*, which is the subject of the second section of this book. In comparison with the Yiddish text, which is colloquial and lively throughout, the French version is a bit flat. It also shows significant cuts, probably by reason of lack of space. Finally, it contains a number of small adaptations and a few inaccuracies. The places where the French text significantly departs from the original or from the Yiddish version have been listed in the footnotes; these departures are identified by means of the abbreviation *F*.

Zvi Kolitz

Yossel Rakover's Appeal To God

I believe in the sun even when it is not shining, I believe in love even when feeling it not; I believe in God even when he is silent.

AN INSCRIPTION ON THE WALL OF A CELLAR IN COLOGNE WHERE A NUMBER OF JEWS HID THEMSELVES FOR THE ENTIRE DURATION OF THE WAR.

In the ruins of the ghetto of Warsaw, among heaps of charred rubbish,[1] there was found, packed tightly into a small bottle, the following testament, written during the ghetto's last hours by a Jew named Yossel Rakover.[2]

5   "*Warsaw, April 28,*[3] *1943.*

"I, Yossel, son of David[4] Rakover of Tarnopol, a Hasid of the Rabbi of Ger and a descendant of the great, pious, and righteous families of Rakover and Meisel, inscribe these lines as the houses of the Warsaw ghetto go up in flames. The house I am in is one of the 10 last unburnt houses remaining. For several hours an unusually heavy artillery barrage has been crashing down on us, and the walls around are disintegrating under the fire. It will not be long before the house I am in is transformed, like almost every other house of the ghetto, into a grave for its defenders. By the dagger-sharp, unusu- 15 ally crimson rays of the sun that strike through the small, half-walled-up window of my room through which we have been shooting at the enemy day and night, I see that it must now be late afternoon, just before sundown, and I cannot regret that this is the last sun that I shall see.[5] All of our notions and emotions have been 20 altered. Death, swift and immediate, seems to us a liberator, sundering our shackles; and beasts of the field in their freedom and gentleness seem to me to be so lovable and dear that I feel a deep pain whenever I hear the evil fiends that lord it over Europe referred to as beasts. It is untrue that the tyrant who rules Europe now[6] has 25 something of the beast in him. He is a typical child of modern man; mankind as a whole spawned him and reared him. He is merely the frankest expression of its innermost, most deeply buried instincts.[7]

"In a forest where I once hid, I encountered a dog one night, sick and hungry,[8] his tail between his legs. Both of us immediately felt 30 the kinship of our situations.[9] He cuddled up to me, buried his head

---

1   *Y adds* and human bones
2   *F omits* 1-4.
3   *F* 23
4   *YF* Yossel
5   18-19 and I cannot ... see: *Y* The sun probably does not know at all how little I regret it that I will not see it again. A peculiar thing has happened to us:
6   the tyrant who rules Europe now: *Y* Hitler
7   *F omits* 12-27 It will ... instincts.
8   *Y adds* maybe crazy as well
9   *YF add* for, after all, the situation of the dogs is not, on the whole, better than ours.

in my lap, and licked my hands. I do not know if I ever cried so much
as that night. I threw my arms around his neck, crying like a baby.
If I say that I envied the animals at that moment, it would not be
remarkable. But what I felt was more than envy. It was shame. I
35 felt ashamed before the dog to be, not a dog, but a man. That is how
matters stand. That is the spiritual level to which we have sunk. Life
is a tragedy, death a savior; man a calamity, the beast an ideal; the
day a horror, the night—relief.

"When my wife, my children and I—six in all—hid in the forest,
40 it was the night[10] and the night alone that concealed us in its bosom.

> Millions of people in the wide, big world, who love the day, the
> sun,[11] and the light, do not know, do not have the slightest no-
> tion,[12] how much darkness and unhappiness it, the sun, has
> brought us. It has become an instrument in the hand of the evil-
> doers, and they have used it as a search-light, to track down the
> footsteps of those who are fleeing.

The day turned us over to our persecutors and murderers. I remember with the most painful clarity the day when the Germans raked
with a hail of fire[13] the thousands of refugees on the highway from
Grodno to Warsaw. As the sun rose, the airplanes zoomed over
45 us. The whole day long they murdered[14] us. In this massacre, my
wife with our seven-months-old child in her arms perished. And
two others of my five remaining children also disappeared that day
without a trace. Their names were David and Yehuda, one was four
years old, the other six.

50 "At sunset, the handful of survivors continued their journey in
the direction of Warsaw, and I, with my three remaining children,
started out to comb the fields and woods at the site of the massacre
in search of the children. The entire night we called for them. Only
echoes replied.[15] I never saw my two children again, and later in a
55 dream was told that[16] they were in God's hands.[17]

---

10 *F omits* the night and
11 *F omits* the sun,
12 *F omits* don't have the slightest notion
13 42-43 I remember ... fire: *YF* How will I ever forget (*F* How could I forget) the day of that hail-shower
     of German fire upon
14 *Y* murdered and murdered
15 53-54: *YF* David! Yehuda! Through the whole night our cries cut, as if with knives, [*F* tore] through
     the deadly silence around us, and a forest-echo, helpless, full of compassion, and heart-rending
     answered our cries with the tone of a funeral oration.
16 *YF* told not to be troubled about them any longer, because
17 *Y* in the hand of *Reboyne-shel-Oylem.*

"My other three children died in the space of a single year[18] in the Warsaw ghetto. Rachel, my daughter of ten, heard that it was possible to find scraps of bread in the public dump outside the ghetto walls. The ghetto was starving at the time, and the people who died
60 of starvation lay in the streets like heaps of rags. The people of the ghetto were prepared to face any death but the death of hunger. Against no death did they struggle so fiercely as against death by starvation.

> That is probably because of this: in times when all desires[19] of a person can be suppressed bit by bit, the will to eat is the only one that remains, even if one wants to die. I have been told about a Jew who was half-starved, who said this to another one: "Ah, how happy I would be, if I could die after eating one more time like a human being!"[20]

"My daughter, Rachel, told me nothing of her plan to steal out
65 of the ghetto, which was punishable by death. She and a girl friend of the same age started out on the perilous journey. She left home under cover of darkness, and at sunrise she and her friend were caught outside the ghetto walls. Nazi ghetto guards, together with dozens of their Polish underlings, at once started in pursuit of these
70 two Jewish children who had dared to venture out to hunt for a piece of bread in a garbage can. People witnessing the chase could not believe their eyes.[21] One might think it was a pursuit of dangerous criminals, that horde of fiends running amok in pursuit of a pair of starved ten-year-old children. They did not endure very long in the
75 unequal match. One of them, my child, running with her last ounce of strength, fell exhausted to the ground, and the Nazis then put a bullet through her head.[22] The other child saved herself, but, driven out of her mind, died two weeks later.
"The fifth child, Yacob, a boy of thirteen, died on his Bar Mitzvah
80 day of tuberculosis.[23] The last child, my fifteen-year-old daughter,

---

18 F omits in the space of a single year
19 F *adds* and all needs
20 like a human being: F sufficiently
21 YF *add* Even in the ghetto that was [F looked] astounding.
22 YF ran her head through [F *adds* with bayonet thrusts].
23 YF *add* His death was a deliverance for him.

Chaya, perished during a *Kinderaktion*[24]—children's operation—that began at sunrise last Rosh Hashona and ended at sundown. That day, before sunset, hundreds of Jewish families lost their children.

"Now my time has come. And like Job, I can say of myself, nor am I the only one that can say it, that I return to the soil naked, as naked as the day of my birth.

"I am forty-three years old, and when I look back on the past I can assert confidently, as confident as a man can be of himself, that I have lived a respectable, upstanding life, my heart full of love for God. I was once blessed with success, but never boasted of it. My possessions were extensive. My house was open to the needy[25]. I served God enthusiastically, and my single request to Him was that He should allow me to worship Him with all my heart, and all my soul, and all my strength.[26]

"I cannot say that my relationship to God has remained unchanged after everything I have lived through, but I can say with absolute certainty that my belief in Him has not changed a hair's breadth. Previously, when I was well off, my relation to God was as to one who granted me a favor for nothing,[27] and I was eternally obliged to Him for it. Now my relations to Him are as to one who owes me something, owes me much,[28] and since I feel so, I believe that I have the right to demand it of Him. But I do not say like Job that God should point out my sin with His finger so that I may know why I deserve this; for greater and saintlier men than I are now firmly convinced that it is not a question of punishing sinners: something entirely different is taking place in the world.[29] More exactly, it is a time when God has veiled His countenance from the world, sacrificing[30] mankind to its wild instincts.

That is why I think that, because those instincts dominate the world, it is unfortunately quite natural that those in whom the

---

24 F *omits Kinderaktion*

25 *YF add* and I was happy whenever I was able to do someone a favor.

26 94-95 Y quotes Deuteronomy 6, 5 in Hebrew.

27 *YF* who favored me unceasingly,

28 F *omits* owes me much

29 F *omits* in the world

30 108-109 Y it is a time of *histeres-ponim.* God has hidden his countenance from the world, and consequently, sacrificed

divine and the pure is alive should be the first victims.[31] That is, perhaps, no comfort. However, since the destiny of our people is determined, not by worldly calculations, but by calculations that are not of this world, spiritual and divine ones, the believer should see in such events a fragment of a great divine reckoning, over against which human tragedies have[32] small importance.

110   This, however, does not mean that the pious members of my people should justify the edict, saying that God and His judgments are correct. For saying that we deserve the blows we have received is to malign ourselves, to desecrate the Holy Name of God's children. And 115 those that desecrate our name desecrate the name of the Lord; God is maligned by our self-deprecation.[33]

In a situation like this, I naturally expect no miracles, nor do I ask Him, my Lord, to show me any mercy. May He treat me with the same indifference with which He treated millions of His people. I 120 am no exception, and I expect no special treatment. I will no longer attempt to save myself, nor flee any more. I will facilitate the work of the fire by moistening my clothing with gasoline. I have three bottles of gasoline left after having emptied several scores over the heads of the murderers. It was one of the finest moments in my life 125 when I did this, and I was shaken with laughter by it. I never dreamed that the death of people, even of enemies —even of such enemies[34] —could cause me such great pleasure. Foolish humanists may say what they choose. Vengeance was and always will be the last means of waging battle and the greatest spiritual release of the 130 oppressed. I had never until now understood the precise meaning of the expression in the Talmud[35] that states: Vengeance is sacred because it is mentioned between two of God's names: A God of vengeance is the Lord.[36] I understand it now. I know now why my

---

31   *F* it is natural that those who preserve the divine and the pure should be the first victims of this domination.

32   *F adds* only

33   113-115 desecrate the name ... self-deprecation: *YF* desecrate the *Shem Hamiforesh....*

34   *F omits* —even of such enemies —

35   *YF* the passage in the *Gemara*

36   *b. Ber.* 33a: "great is vengeance since it has been set between two names, as it says, *God of Vengeance, O Lord* [Ps 94, 1]."

heart is so overjoyed at remembering that for thousands of years we have been calling our Lord a God of Vengeance: A God of Venge-
35 ance is our Lord.[37]

> Now that I am in a position to see life with particularly clear eyes —something only rarely given to people before death—it seems to me that there is a fundamental difference between our God and the God of the Gentiles: our God is a God of vengeance, and our Torah is full of death penalties for the smallest[38] sins. And yet it was enough for the Sanhedrin, the highest tribunal of our people in its land, to sentence a person to death once in seventy years to have the judges considered murderers.[39] On the other hand, the God of the Gentiles has commanded to love every creature made in his image, and in his name our blood has been poured out for almost two thousand years.
> Yes, I have spoken of vengeance.

We have had only a few opportunities to witness true vengeance. When we did, however, it was so good, so worthwhile I felt such profound happiness, so terribly fortunate[40] that it seemed an entirely new life was springing up in me. A tank had suddenly broken into our street. It was bombarded with flam-
40 ing bottles of gasoline from all the embattled houses. They failed to hit their target, however, and the tank continued to approach. My friends and I waited until the tank was almost upon us. Then, through the half bricked-up window, we suddenly attacked. The tank soon burst into flames, and six blazing Nazis jumped out. Ah,
45 how they burned! They burned like the Jews they had set on fire. But they shrieked more. Jews do not shriek. They welcome death like a savior. The Warsaw ghetto perished in battle. It went down shooting, struggling, blazing, but not shrieking!
"I have three more bottles of gasoline. They are as precious to
50 me as wine to a drunkard. After pouring one over my clothes, I will place the paper on which I write these lines in the empty bottle and hide it among the bricks filling the window of this room. If anyone

---

37   Y *E-l nikomes Hashem.* F *El Nekamoth Adonaï.*
38   F venial
39   Cf. *m. Mak.* 1:20; *b. Mak.* 7a.
40   F *omits* so terribly fortunate

ever finds it and reads it, he will, perhaps, understand the emotions of a Jew, one of millions, who died forsaken by the God in whom he believed unshakeably. I will let the two other bottles explode on the heads of the murderers when my last moment comes.

"There were twelve of us in this room at the outbreak of the rebellion. For nine days we battled against the enemy. All eleven of my comrades have fallen, dying silently in battle, including the small boy of about five—who came here only God knows how and who now lies dead near me, with his face wearing the kind of smile that appears on children's faces when dreaming peacefully—even this child died with the same epic calm as his older comrades. It happened early this morning. Most of us were dead already. The boy scaled the heap of corpses to catch a glimpse of the outside world through the window. He stood beside me in that position for several minutes. Suddenly he fell backwards, rolling down the pile of corpses, and lay like a stone. On his small, pale forehead, between the locks of black hair, there was a spattering of blood.[41]

"Up until yesterday morning, when the enemy launched a concentrated barrage against this stronghold, one of the last in the ghetto, at sunrise, every one of us was still alive, although five were wounded. During yesterday and today, all of them fell, one after the other, one on top of the other, watching and firing until shot to death. I have no more ammunition, apart from the three bottles of gasoline. From the floors of the house above still come frequent shots, but they can hold out no more hope for me, for by all signs the stairway has been razed by the shell fire, and I think the house is about to collapse. I write these lines lying on the floor. Around me lie my dead comrades. I look into their faces, and it seems to me that a quiet but mocking[42] irony animates them, as if they were saying to me, 'A little patience, you foolish man, another few minutes and everything will become clear to you too.' This irony is particularly noticeable on the face of the small boy lying near my right hand as if he were asleep. His small mouth is drawn into a smile exactly as if he were laughing, and I, who still live and feel and think—it seems

---

41 YF *add*: a bullet in the head.
42 F *omits* quiet but mocking

to me that he is laughing at me. He laughs with that quiet but eloquent, penetrating laughter so characteristic of the wise, speaking of knowledge with the ignorant who believe they know everything. Yes, he is omniscient now. Everything is clear to the boy now. He even knows why he was born, but had to die so soon, why he died only five years after his birth. And even if he does not know why, he knows at least that it is entirely unimportant and insignificant whether or not he knows it, in the light of the revelation of that godly majesty of the better world he now inhabits, in the arms of his murdered parents to whom he has returned. In an hour or two I will make the same discovery. Unless my face is eaten by the flames, a similar smile may also rest on it after my death. Meanwhile, I still live, and before my death I wish to speak to my Lord as a living man, a simple, living person who had the great but tragic honor of being a Jew.

"I am proud that I am a Jew not in spite of the world's treatment of us, but precisely because of this treatment.[43] I should be ashamed to belong to the people who spawned and raised the criminals who are responsible for the deeds that have been perpetrated against us.

"I am proud to be a Jew because it is an *art* to be a Jew, because it is difficult[44] to be a Jew. It is no art to be an Englishman, an American, or a Frenchman. It may be easier, more comfortable, to be one of them, but not more honorable. Yes, it is an honor to be a Jew.

"I believe that to be a Jew means to be a fighter, an everlasting swimmer against the turbulent, criminal human current. The Jew is a hero, a martyr, a saint. You, our enemies, declare that we are bad? I believe that we are better and finer than you, but even if we were worse—I should like to see how you would look in our place!

"I am happy to belong to the unhappiest of all peoples of the world, whose precepts represent[45] the loftiest and most beautiful of all morality and laws. These immortal precepts which we possess have now been even more sanctified and immortalized by the fact that they have been so debased and insulted by the enemies of the Lord.

---

43 219-220 *YF* I am proud to be a Jew, not to spite the world because of its attitude toward us, but actually [*F* precisely] for the sake of that attitude.
44 *YF add* oh how difficult!
45 *YF* whose Torah represents

"I believe that to be a Jew is an inborn trait. One is born a Jew exactly as one is born an artist. It is impossible to be released from being a Jew. That is our godly attribute that has made us a chosen
225   people. Those who do not understand this will never understand the higher meaning of our martyrdom.

Nothing more whole than a broken heart, a great rabbi has said,[46] and there is no people more chosen than a people continually persecuted.[47]

If I ever doubted that God once designated us as the chosen people, I would believe now that our tribulations have made us the chosen one.

"I believe in You, God of Israel, even though You have done
230   everything to stop me from believing in You. I believe in Your laws even if I cannot excuse Your actions. My relationship to You is not the relationship of a slave to his master but rather that of a pupil to his teacher. I bow my head before Your greatness, but will not kiss the lash with which You strike me.

I love Him, but I love His Torah[48] more, and even if I had deceived myself in His regard,[49] I would nonetheless observe His Torah.[50] God means religion, but His Torah means a way of life, and the more we die for such a way of life, the more immortal it becomes.

235   "You say, perhaps, that we have sinned, O Lord? It must surely be true. And therefore we are punished? I can understand that too. But I should like You to tell me—*Is there any sin in the world deserving of such punishment as the punishment we have received?*

"You assert that You will yet repay our enemies? I am con-
240   vinced of it. Repay them without mercy? I have no doubt of that either. I should like You to tell me, however—*Is there any punishment in the world capable of compensating for the crimes that have been committed against us?*

"You say, I know, that it is no longer a question of sin and

---

46   Nahman of Bratslav (1772-1811); the saying is quoted in Arthur Green, *Tormented Master*, p. 148.
47   F *omits the entire expansion.*
48   F *even more*
49   F *and even if I had been deceived by him and, as it were, disenchanted*
50   F *the precepts of His Torah*

245 punishment, but rather a situation in which Your countenance is veiled, in which humanity is abandoned to its evil instincts. I should like to ask You, O Lord—and this question burns in me like a consuming fire —*What more, O, what more must transpire before You unveil Your countenance again to the world?*

250 "I want to say to You[51] that now, more than in any previous period of our eternal path of agony, we, we the tortured, humiliated, buried alive, and burned alive, we the insulted, the object of mockery, we who have been murdered by the millions, we have the right to know: *What are the limits of Your forebearance?*

255 "I should like to say something more: Do not put the rope[52] under too much strain, lest, alas, it may snap. The test to which You have put us is so severe, so unbearably severe, that You should— You must —forgive those members of Your people who, in their misery, have turned from You.

260 "Forgive those who have turned from You in their misery, but also those who have turned from You in their happiness. You have transformed our life into such a frightful, perpetual struggle that the cowards among us have been forced to flee from it; and what is happiness but a place of refuge for cowards? Do not chastise them 265 for it. One does not strike cowards, but has mercy on them. Have mercy on *them*, rather than *us*, O Lord.

"Forgive those who have desecrated Your name, who have gone over to the service of other gods, who have become indifferent to You. You have castigated them so severely that they no longer 270 believe that You are their Father, that they have any Father at all.

"I tell You this because I do believe in You, believe in You more strongly than ever, because now I know that You are my Lord, because after all You are not, You cannot after all[53] be the God of those whose deeds are the most horrible expression of ungodliness.[54]

275 "If You are not *my* Lord, then whose Lord are You? The Lord of the murderers?

"If those that hate me and murder me are so benighted, so evil, what then am I if not the person who reflects something of Your light, of Your goodness?

---

51 YF *add* clearly and frankly
52 F the bow
53 F *omits* after all
54 Y of militant godlessness   F of a militant absence of God

280   "I cannot extol You for the deeds that You tolerate. I bless You and extol You, however, for the very fact of Your existence, for Your awesome mightiness.

> which must be so immense that even what is happening now makes no impression on You! And precisely because You are so great and I so small, I pray You, I warn You for the sake of Your name:[55] stop underscoring Your greatness by allowing the unfortunate to be stricken! I am not asking You either to strike the guilty. It is in the dreadful nature of the events that they will eventually strike themselves, since in our being killed the conscience of the world has been killed, since a world has been murdered in the murder of Israel. The world will be devoured by its own evil, it will drown in its own blood.

"The murderers themselves have already passed sentence on themselves and will never escape it; but may You carry out a doubly
285 severe sentence on those who are condoning the murder.

"Those that condemn murder orally, but rejoice at it in their hearts... Those who meditate in their foul hearts: It is fitting, after all, to say that he is evil, this tyrant, but he carries out a bit of work for us for which we will always be grateful to him!

290   "It is written in your Torah that a thief should be punished more severely than a brigand, in spite of the fact that a thief does not attack his victim physically and merely attempts to take his possessions stealthily.

"The reason for this is that the brigand in attacking his victim in
295 broad daylight, shows no more fear of man than of God. The thief on the other hand fears man, but not God. His punishment, therefore, is greater.

"I should be satisfied if you dealt with the murderers as with brigands, for their attitude towards you and towards us is the same.[56]
300   "But those who are silent in the face of murder, those who have no fear of You, but fear what people might say (fools! they are unaware that the people will say nothing!), those who express their

---

55   *F omits* for the sake of Your name

sympathy with the drowning man but refuse to rescue him—punish them, O Lord, punish them, I implore You, like the thief, with a
305 doubly-severe sentence!

"Death can wait no longer. From the floors above me, the firing becomes weaker by the minute. The last defenders of this stronghold are now falling, and with them falls and perishes the great, beautiful, and God-fearing Jewish part of Warsaw. The sun is about
310 to set, and I thank God that I will never see it again. Fire lights the small window, and the bit of sky that I can see is flooded with red like a waterfall of blood. In about an hour at the most I will be with the rest of my family and with the millions of other stricken members of my people in that better world where there are no more doubts.
315 "I die peacefully, but not complacently; persecuted, but not enslaved; embittered, but not cynical; a believer, but not a supplicant; a lover of God, but no blind amen-sayer of His.

"I have followed Him even when He repulsed me. I have followed His commandments even when He castigated me for it; I have
320 loved Him and I love Him even when He has hurled me to the earth, tortured me to death, made me an object of shame and ridicule.

"My rabbi would frequently tell the story of a Jew who fled from the Spanish Inquisition with his wife and child, striking out in a small boat over the stormy sea until he reached a rocky island. A
325 flash of lightning[57] killed his wife; a storm rose and hurled his son into the sea. Then, as lonely as a stone, naked, barefoot, lashed by the storm and terrified by the thunder and lightning, hands turned up to God, the Jew, again setting out on his journey through the wastes of the rocky island, turned to God with the following words:
330 " 'God of Israel, I have fled to this place in order to worship You without molestation, to obey Your commandments and sanctify Your name. You, however, have done everything to make me stop believing in You. Now, lest it seem to You that You will succeed by these tribulations in driving me from the right path, I notify You, my
335 God and the God of my father, *that it will not avail you in the least.* You may insult me, You may castigate me, You may take from me all that I cherish and hold dear in the world, You may torture me to death— *I* will believe in *You*, *I* will always love *You!*'[58]

---

56 YF *add* and they make no secret of their murders and crimes.
57 YF *add* his hair dishevelled
58 Y *adds* always, You alone, just for spite!

"And these are my last words to You, my wrathful God: nothing
340 will avail You in the least. You have done everything to make me
renounce You, to make me lose my faith in You, but I die exactly as
I have lived, crying:[59]

"Eternally praised be the God of the dead, the God of vengeance, of truth and of law, Who will soon show His face to the world
345 again and shake its foundations with His almighty voice.

"Hear, O Israel, the Lord our God the Lord is One.

"Into your hands, O Lord, I consign my soul."

---

59   YF *omit* crying: YF *add* with a faith in You firm as a rock.

Reflections

The remainder of this section must be devoted to three brief reflections. First, there are two theological issues to raise. After that, we must once more turn our attention to the expansions found in the Yiddish version of *Yossel Rakover's Appeal to God*.

Israel's Suffering as Proof of Divine Election

Besides being a monument to one of Judaism's—and humanity's—most heart-rending moments, Zvi Kolitz' story makes a fundamental theological statement of principle: the living God is associated, in a very particular way, with suffering.

Negatively, Yossel states that it is *illegitimate* to interpret the immense suffering undergone by the innocent Jews as a punishment for sin, coming from an angry God. In no way do the Jews *deserve* the suffering that is inflicted on them. Thus Yossel writes in his testament:

> I do not say like Job that God should point out my sin with His finger so that I may know why I deserve this; for greater and saintlier men than I are now firmly convinced that it is not a question of punishing sinners: something entirely different is taking place in the world. [...] God has veiled His countenance from the world, sacrificing mankind to its wild instincts [103-109].

In Kolitz' story, far from being angry at those who are suffering, God *positively* associates with them. In fact, it is precisely their suffering that identifies the Jews as God's chosen people:

> I am proud that I am a Jew not in spite of the world's treatment of us, but precisely because of this treatment. I should be ashamed to belong to the people who spawned and raised the criminals who are responsible for the deeds that have been perpetrated against us [202-206].

And:

> I do believe in You, believe in You more strongly than ever, be-

cause now I know that You are my Lord, because after all You are
not, You cannot after all be the God of those whose deeds are the
most horrible expression of ungodliness.

If You are not *my* Lord, then whose Lord are You? The Lord
of the murderers?

If those that hate me and murder me are so benighted, so evil,
what then am I if not the person who reflects something of Your
light, of Your goodness? [271-279].

In this way, the Jews, who insist on living in obedience to the
Torah despite their being abandoned by God, are identified—*by contrast*,[7] that is, by their very suffering—as the representatives of the
living God in the midst of an evil, lawless world:

If I ever doubted that God once designated us as the chosen
people, I would believe now that our tribulations have made us
the chosen one [226-228].

In all of this, Kolitz is doing two things. First of all, he is calling
on Jews to recapture the core of their faith in God: not a fair-weather
faith in a fair-weather God, but a faith *proven* by fidelity to a God who
leads the chosen people by *testing* it. This is a fundamental element
in the Jewish profession of faith in God. As such, it must be of fundamental importance to Christians, too. Hence, it is one of the theological issues that must be raised again, in the third section of this
book.

But secondly, in associating true faith in God with suffering,
Kolitz is squarely challenging Christians, too. He does so by suggesting a shocking parallel.

Israel's Suffering as a Challenge to Christians

To Christian ears, the last line of the story, taken from Psalm 31 (verse
5), is unmistakable: the words "Into your hands, O Lord, I consign
my soul" are the last words of the dying Jesus in the gospel according
to Luke (Lk 23, 46). In that Gospel, Jesus is identified as God's chosen
one precisely by his total fidelity and abandon to God in the midst
of dereliction and suffering. The Gospel of Mark would appear to
make this point explicitly: the centurion who proclaims the dead
Jesus "a Son of God" does so when he has seen "how he cried out in

this fashion and died" (Mk 15, 39). Yossel Rakover, in Kolitz' mind, is to be associated with this Christ, suffering in this particular fashion.

In this way, Kolitz' story makes the same provocative statement as Marc Chagall's *White Crucifixion*. In this magnificent painting, the crucified Christ is surrounded by scenes from pogroms—Jews killed, hunted down, and driven away, synagogues burning, Torah-scrolls desecrated.

To a Jew, this is the world turned upside down: the *cross*, traditionally the sign and symbol of persecution, has become the *emblem of compassion*. But for Christians, too, the tables are turned. In Chagall's painting, far from being the *victim of Jewish rejection*—as he is depicted even by the Gospels—*Jesus Christ is on the victims' side*. Naked and exposed, his only covering is the vestment worn by Jews at prayer. He has become the *exemplar* of the suffering, rejected Jews who have none but God to commit themselves to.

Christ rejected by whom? In Chagall's painting, as in Kolitz' story, that answer is not explicitly given; still, it is very much implied. In the persons of the persecuted Jews, Christ is rejected by the very people who, at least by tradition, acknowledge him as their Savior. In what way do they reject him? Kolitz answers that question very explicitly: Christ is rejected by those who actively inflict violence on the Jews, but even more insidiously, by the self-centered, irresponsible, and apathetic Christians who are the silent accomplices of that violence [286-289; 300-305].[8]

This raises a second important theological issue. Picturing Jesus Christ as associated with the persecuted Jews amounts to a major theological challenge to the traditional Christian imagination; can, or must, Christians recognize the suffering Jesus as the associate of suffering Jewry?[9] And if so, does this change of imagination require a reinterpretation of Christian doctrine about the person of Jesus Christ and of Christianity's relationship with Judaism? This theological question, too, must come up for discussion in the third section of this book.

The Agenda of the Expansions in the Yiddish Version

There is a third issue to be briefly discussed at this point: the meaning of the expansions found in the Yiddish version of Kolitz' story.

Within the framework of the present book, these expansions derive their importance from the fact that they are part of the version of *Yossel Rakover's Appeal to God* that happened to come to the attention of Emmanuel Levinas. Curiously, the expansions turn out to be crucial to Emmanuel Levinas' commentary: out of the six quotations from the story found in *Aimer la Thora plus que Dieu*, as many as three are, in whole or in part, taken from the inserted passages.

Of the seven expansions, two do little more than adding telling, dramatic detail: the reference to the sun as a searchlight in the hands of the Nazis [at line 40], and the anecdote about the irrepressible will to eat during a famine [at line 63]. The other five expansions are more important, in that they successfully reinforce four of the story's *theological themes*. First of all, the conviction that *suffering identifies Israel as God's people* is given extra depth by a reference to God's mysterious design [at line 109], and by the application of Rabbi Nahman of Bratslav's wonderful saying "There is nothing as whole as a broken heart"[10] to the chosen people [at line 226—a feature omitted by the French translation]. Secondly, Israel's suffering is made to serve, not only as a stunning *revelation of God's transcendence*, experienced as cold indifference, but also as a *revelation as well as an indictment of the suicidal evil of the world* [at line 282]. Thirdly, the conviction that present *suffering serves to glorify the beauty and the nobility of the Torah* is intensified [at line 234]. Fourthly and finally, *Israel's close association with God as God's own chosen people* is radicalized by means of the theme of divine Vengeance, and turned into an indignant *rejection of the Christians' claim that their God is a God of Love* [at line 135].

Not surprisingly, these four points are among Emmanuel Levinas' principal themes. In the next section we must discuss them.

TWO

To Love the Torah More than God

Preliminaries

Introduction: Emmanuel Levinas on Judaism and Christianity

On Friday, April 29, 1955, twelve years after the Warsaw ghetto was experiencing the eleventh day of its desperate struggle, the Lithuanian-French Jewish philosopher Emmanuel Levinas delivered an address. He did so in a radio program devoted to Judaism, entitled *Écoute Israel* ("Hear, Israel," after the opening words of the *Shema*, the Jewish profession of faith; cf. Deut 6, 4ff.). What Levinas read on the air was a commentary on an anonymous story he had found, just over six weeks before, in the March 15 edition of the Zionist newspaper published in Paris, *La Terre Retrouvée*. As far as Levinas knew, the story had been translated by Arnold Mandel from an anonymous Yiddish original.

The editors of *La Terre Retrouvée* had provided the following glowing introduction:

> Arnold Mandel has translated, from the Yiddish, a text which, it seems to us, is extraordinarily lofty in thought and feeling, and agonizing in its emotionality. We would not want to deprive our readers of this heartfelt cry, in which anger, revolt, and—despite everything—unshakable love of God come to expression, in Job's tone of voice, discovered anew.
>
> This text, by an unknown author, appeared in the Yiddish-language Israeli review «Die Goldene Kaït».

In the story, Levinas had been happy to recognize what he considered to be the true spirit of traditional, mature Judaism—the religion he was to characterize a few years later as "a religion of adults."[1]

In giving the address, however, Levinas obviously wanted to do something more than give expression to his deep satisfaction as a Jew; he also meant to make a statement that would be provocative and controversial. He conveyed his intention by contradicting the *Shema* in the very title of his talk. Instead of taking the text of Deuteronomy (Deut 6, 5): "You shall love the Lord your God" for his title, he wrote *"Aimer la Thora plus que Dieu"*—To Love the Torah more than God."[2] Eight years later, in 1963, when the text first appeared in print, in a collection of shorter essays entitled *Difficile liberté: Essais sur le Judaïsme*—"Difficult Freedom: Essays on Judaism"—Levinas confirmed his original intention: the radio broadcast was bluntly billed, along with a cluster of other essays, as a "polemic."

A few words by way of introduction. For Levinas, the Holocaust ineluctably raises the two fundamental, intimately related and hence inseparable issues of the religious life, and indeed, the truly human life: faith in God and ethical responsibility. After Auschwitz, this means, rather more specifically and urgently, the very *possibility of faith* in a just God, and the very *capacity of human persons to take responsibility* for a just world.

Far from inviting just another brave academic discussion, this question must become thick and concrete to the point of near-intractability. Raised in the wake of the Holocaust, it must put both Gentiles and Jews on the spot. How can the surviving Jewish community, having barely escaped extermination for no other reason than being Jewish, recapture its faith in a just God or persevere in it, or perhaps even deepen it? And how can the international Christian—or at least post-Christian—commonwealth, having once failed, in the Holocaust, to live up to its responsibility to all of humanity, still claim to be a community that believes in the living God? After all, do Christians not profess faith in a God whose compassionate love, revealed in Jesus Christ, embraces friend and enemy, and seeks the salvation of all (cf. 1 Tim 2, 4)? Or at the very least, does the secularized, residually Christian West not acknowledge God as Creator, in whose name all that is human deserves to be equally respected? And finally, is it possible for Jews and Gentiles alike so to absorb the shock of the Holocaust as to draw from it a wisdom reliable enough to support another attempt at building a world that is just, or at least more just, and if so, how?

For Levinas, these questions do become thick and concrete. And the answer that he gives is far from cool, impartial, or tolerant. His affirmation of the possibility of faith in God and of human responsibility takes the shape of a passionate *apologia* for Judaism—a Judaism, he insists, that has been misunderstood and misinterpreted and disdained from time immemorial by Christians, in what I have called an "asymmetrical" fashion. Levinas wants religion and responsibility—faith and justice; and in the name of faith and justice, he also wants symmetry, not asymmetry, between Christianity and Judaism.

Judaism Independent of, and Superior to, Christianity

There are two levels to Levinas' argument. On a first level, he argues that Judaism can maintain itself *independently of Christianity*, both as a way of true worship and as a responsible form of humanism. In "To Love the Torah More than God," Levinas maintains that Judaism is whole and integral in itself; there is nothing preparatory or provisional about it; it "has nothing to prefigure"; in and of itself, it is a demanding, "difficult journey," and it stands in no need of any Christian fulfillment to vindicate or improve it. And with a pointed denial of Jesus' word about the true worshipers of God, addressed, in the fourth Gospel (Jn 4, 23), to the Samaritan woman at the well, Levinas indicates that Judaism's journey is "already being undertaken in spirit and truth" [119]. Consequently, Judaism demands that it be understood on its own terms, in symmetry with Christianity, and not just in a onesided, asymmetrical relation to it.

But there is a second level to Levinas' contention as well. Not satisfied with mere symmetry, he argues that there are grounds, both philosophical and theological, upon which Judaism can justly claim to be a religion *superior to Christianity*. Levinas bases this decisive contention on the argument that Judaism is marked, *in a way Christianity is not*, both by the full acknowledgment of God's transcendent majesty and by a disciplined, fully mature, conscientious sense of the human responsibility in behalf of humanity and the world. As he phrases it, Judaism is "an integral and austere humanism, coupled with difficult worship! And from the other point of view, a worship that coincides with the exaltation of Man" [158-160].

This is a serious critique, coming from a serious mind. When it was first voiced, it addressed not only certain forms of routine Judaism—of the kind that have lost touch with Judaism's deeper tradition [3-5]—but also, and especially, the routine Christianity of the average French radio audience, as well as the convictions and prejudices of the existentialist intelligentsia, Christian or otherwise, of the mid-fifties [21-25]. I want to suggest that it can still speak to American Christians, whether routine or sophisticated, today. If I am not mistaken, it can also address modern American Jews. Let us read it, then, with the respect it deserves.

Emmanuel Levinas

To Love the Torah More Than God

AMONG THE RECENT PUBLICATIONS devoted to Judaism in the West, there are a great many beautiful texts. Talent is not a problem in Europe. Rarely, however, are the texts real. Over the past one hundred years, Hebrew learning has faded, and we have lost touch
5 with our sources. What learning is still being produced is no longer based on an intellectual tradition; it remains self-taught and untutored, even when it is not improvised. And what worse corruption can befall an author than being read only by people who know less than he does! With none to check them, none to put them in their
10 places, authors tend to mistake the lack of counter-pressure for freedom, and this freedom for the touch of genius. Small wonder that the reading public remains skeptical; for them, Judaism, with its few million unrepentant adherents left in the world, is no more than a matter of quibbling over religious observances—something unin-
15 teresting and unimportant.

I have just read a text which is both beautiful and real—as real as only fiction can be. An anonymous author published it in an Israeli journal; it was translated for *La Terre Retrouvée*—the Zionist paper in Paris—under the title *Yossel, son of Yossel Rakover of Tarnopol, speaks*
20 *to God*, by Mr. Arnold Mandel, who, it would appear, had read it with deep emotion. The text deserves even more. It conveys an intellectual attitude that reflects something better than the reading habits of intellectuals—something superior to the handful of concepts borrowed, for instance, from Simone Weil, who, as everyone in Paris
25 knows, is the latest fad in religious terminology. What this text provides is Jewish learning modestly understated, yet full of assurance; it represents a deep, authentic experience of the spiritual life.

The text presents itself as a document written during the last few hours of the Resistance of the Warsaw Ghetto. The narrator has
30 been a witness to all those horrors; he has lost his young children under brutal circumstances. As his family's last survivor, and that for only a few more moments, he bequeaths to us his final thoughts. A literary fiction—certainly, but a fiction that affords each one of us, survivors, a dizzying view of ourselves and our lives.

I am not going to recount that whole tale, even though the world has learned nothing and forgotten everything. I pass when I am asked to stage the Passion of Passions as if it were a show; I refuse to derive any author's or play director's glory from those inhuman cries. They resound and reverberate, never to be silenced, through the everlasting ages. Let us listen only to the thought that articulates itself in them.

What is the meaning of the suffering of the innocent? Does it not witness to a world without God, to an earth where only humanity determines the measure of Good and Evil? The simplest, most ordinary response would indeed be: to draw the conclusion that there is no god. This would also be the healthiest response for all those who, thus far, had believed in a rather elementary god, who awarded prizes, imposed sanctions, or pardoned mistakes, and who, in his goodness, treated people like perpetual children. But what kind of limited spirit, what kind of strange magician did you project as the inhabitant of your heaven—you, who today state that heaven is deserted? And why are you still looking, underneath an empty heaven, for a world that makes sense and is good?

Yossel son of Yossel experiences, with renewed vigor, underneath an empty heaven, certainty about God. For his finding himself thus alone allows him to feel, on his shoulders, all of God's responsibilities. On the road that leads to the one and only God, there is a way station without God. True monotheism must frame answers to the legitimate demands of atheism. An adult person's God reveals himself precisely in the emptiness of the child's heaven. That is (according to Yossel ben Yossel) the moment when God withdraws himself from the world and veils his countenance. "He has sacrificed humankind to its wild instincts," says our text. "... And because those instincts dominate the world, it is natural that those who preserve the divine and the pure should be the first victims of this domination."[1]

God veiling his countenance: I think this is neither a theolo-

---

1   *Yossel Rakover's Appeal to God,* line 109 and expansion.

gian's abstraction nor a poetic image. It is the hour when the just person has nowhere to go in the outside world; when no institution
70 affords him protection; when even the comforting sense of the divine presence, experienced in a childlike person's piety, is withdrawn; when the only victory available to the individual lies in his conscience, which necessarily means: in suffering. This is the specifically Jewish meaning of suffering—one that never takes on the
75 quality of a mystical expiation for the sins of the world. The condition in which victims find themselves in a disordered world, that is to say, in a world where goodness does not succeed in being victorious, is suffering. This reveals a God who, while refusing to manifest himself in any way as a help, directs his appeal to the full matur-
80 ity of the integrally responsible person.

But by the same token this God who veils His countenance and who abandons the just person, unvictorious, to his own justice—this faraway God—comes from inside. That is the intimacy that coincides, in one's conscience, with the pride of being Jewish, of being
85 concretely, historically, altogether mindlessly, a part of the Jewish people. "To be a Jew means ... to be an everlasting swimmer against the turbulent, criminal human current. ... I am happy to belong to the unhappiest people in the world, to the people whose Torah represents the loftiest and most beautiful of all laws and moralities."[2]
90 Intimacy with this virile God is attained in passing an ultimate test. Because I belong to the suffering Jewish people, the faraway God becomes *my God*. "Now I know that you are truly my God, for you cannot possibly be the God of those whose deeds are the most horrible expression of a militant absence of God."[3] The just person's
95 suffering for the sake of a justice that fails to triumph is concretely lived out in the form of Judaism. Israel—historical, carnal Israel—once again becomes a religious category.

God veiling his countenance and recognized as present and intimate: is he possible? Or are we dealing with a metaphysical
100 construct, with a paradoxical *salto mortale* in the style of Kierkegaard? I think something very different manifests itself here,

---

2   *Yossel Rakover's Appeal to God*, lines 211-212, 216-218.
3   *Yossel Rakover's Appeal to God*, lines 272-274.

namely, the characteristic features of Judaism: the relationship between God and the human person is not an emotional communion within the context of the love of an incarnate God, but a relationship between minds that is mediated by teaching, by the Torah. The guarantee that there is a living God in our midst is precisely a word of God that is not incarnate. Trust in a God who does not reveal himself through any worldly authority can rest only on inner clarity and on the quality of a teaching. There is nothing blind about it, much to the credit of Judaism. Hence this phrase of Yossel ben Yossel, which is the high point of the entire monologue, echoing the whole Talmud: "I love him, but I love his Torah even more. ... And even if I had been deceived by him and, as it were, disenchanted, I would nonetheless observe the precepts of the Torah."[4] Blasphemy? Well, in any case a protection against the folly of a direct contact with the Sacred, not based on reasonable grounds. But above all, a trust not based on the triumph of any institution, but on the inner clarity of the morality conveyed by the Torah. A difficult journey, this, already being undertaken in spirit and truth, and which has nothing to prefigure! Simone Weil, you have never understood anything about the Torah! "Our God is a God of vengeance," says Yossel ben Yossel, "and our Torah is full of death penalties for venial sins. And yet it was enough for the Sanhedrin, the highest tribunal of our people in its land, to sentence a person to death once in seventy years to have the judges considered murderers. On the other hand, the God of the Gentiles has commanded to love every creature made in his image, and in his name our blood has been poured out for almost two thousand years."[5]

The true humanity of Man and his virile tenderness come into the world along with the severe words of a demanding God; the spiritual becomes present, not by way of palpable presence, but by absence; God is concrete, not by means of incarnation, but by means of the Law; and his majesty is not the felt experience of his sacred

---

4   *Yossel Rakover's Appeal to God*, expansion at line 234.
5   *Yossel Rakover's Appeal to God,*, expansion at line 135.

135 mystery. His majesty does not provoke fear and trembling, but fills us with higher thoughts. To veil his countenance in order to de-mand—in a superhuman way—everything of Man, to have created Man capable of responding, of turning to his God as a creditor and not all the time as a debtor: *that* is truly divine majesty! After all, a
140 creditor is one who has faith *par excellence*, but he is not going to resign himself to the subterfuges of the debtor. Our monologue opens and closes with this refusal to settle for resignation. Capable of trusting in an absent God, Man is also the adult who can take the measure of his own weakness: if the heroic situation in which he
145 stands validates the world, it also puts it in jeopardy. Matured by a faith derived from the Torah, he blames God for his unbounded Majesty and his excessive demands. He will love him in spite of God's every attempt to discourage his love. But, Yossel ben Yossel cries out, "do not put the bow under too much strain."[6] Religious
150 life cannot come to fruition in this heroic situation. God must unveil his countenance, justice and power must find each other again, just institutions are needed on this earth. But only the person who rec-ognized the veiled God can demand his revelation. How vigorous the dialectic by which the equality between God and Man is estab-
155 lished right at the heart of their incommensurability!

  And thus we are as far removed from the warm, almost palpable communion with the divine as from the desperate pride of the athe-ist. An integral and austere humanism, coupled with difficult worship! And from the other point of view, a worship that coin-
160 cides with the exaltation of Man! A personal God, one God alone: that is not revealed as quickly as a slide shown in a dark room! The text I have commented on shows how ethics and the order of first principles combine to establish a personal relationship worthy of the name. To love the Torah more than God—this means precisely: to
165 find a personal God against whom it is possible to revolt, that is to say, one for whom one can die.

---

6   *Yossel Rakover's Appeal to God*, lines 255-256.

Reflections

In trying to understand this impressive essay, it is important, first of all, to understand its author's *intentions*. Levinas emphasizes that his essay is not to be taken as an attempt at theatrical *self-glorification* on his part, based on his association with the sufferings of the countless Jews murdered in the Holocaust. Nor, he continues, is it an exercise—an exercise that would be futile in any event—in *admonition*: those who have not learned from the anguish of the Holocaust the first time around will not learn from a dramatic replay of it. It is simply an exercise in *understanding* [35-41]. The fact of the matter is, however, that such an understanding has serious obstacles to contend with.

Ignorance About Judaism

The first obstacle to a true understanding of Judaism is *ignorance* — ignorance on the part of both Jews and non-Jews. Levinas explains, in a characteristically self-critical vein, how Jews over the past century have lost touch with their tradition.[3] As a result, self-styled Jewish authors can write anything they want and get away with it. Having become ignorant of their own tradition, modern Jews are unreliable critics and hence, gullible readers who will even applaud mediocre authors as long as they posture as talented [3-11].

Christians are equally ignorant about Judaism. In the nineteen fifties, this was very well demonstrated, in Levinas' view, by the wave of popularity, among the Paris intelligentsia, of the writings of Simone Weil. Levinas very much recognized the intelligence, magnanimity, and even saintliness of Simone Weil, but he could not but deplore her utter misconstrual of the Hebrew Scriptures.[4] A few words by way of explanation.

Simone Weil, born in Paris in 1909 into a well-to-do agnostic Jewish household, had given evidence of a brilliant philosophical mind at an early age. A retiring soul with an indubitably mystical bent and possessed of a heroic if somewhat morbid penchant for identification with human suffering of every kind, she set out on a restless career involving much study as well as a succession of idealistic pursuits. She left Nazi-occupied France in 1942 and after a brief stay in the United States moved to the South of England, where she died of tuberculosis in 1943 at the age of 34. Though increasingly fascinated, and indeed absorbed, by the person of Jesus Christ, she was never able to get herself to join the Catholic Church. She stayed on its threshold, possibly out of fear that joining the Church would cut her off from the rest of humanity. Levinas, in one of his essays, suggests a different reason: quite conceivably, Simone Weil, haunted by Platonist clarity,[5] may have thought that the Church, in "imposing the Jewish Scriptures everywhere" was still too much tied, to her taste, to the (unspiritual) "letter" at the expense of the spirit.[6] Whatever her reasons for not joining the Catholic Church, Simone Weil had come to the notice of the French Catholic philosopher Gustave Thibon and of the learned theologian Père Joseph-Marie Perrin, O.P.,[7] who together decided to sponsor the publication of her writings, starting in 1948.[8]

Needless to say, the existentialist mood of the nineteen fifties, with its fondness for *personal authenticity* and *personal choice* as the principal, and indeed the sole, sources of moral value, enhanced the appeal of Simone Weil's writings. Catholic thinkers with existentialist leanings were even more fascinated by the fact that it was a young *Jewish* woman who had written with such abandon about her Christian faith being the crowning grace of her Jewish descent as well as the most deeply personal motivating force behind her commitments.

Levinas remains unimpressed. To him, the popularity of Simone Weil is little more than another wave of ignorance *à la mode*. What is happening is simply this: Catholics ignorant of Judaism are fashionably admiring a talented and even heroic young Jewish woman who was as ignorant about Judaism in her day as they are now—a Jewish woman, moreover, who had turned to Christianity on grounds that were both philosophically and biblically dubious.

Dubious grounds. That phrase sums up the second, and major, set of obstacles to a true understanding of Judaism. Christianity is so accustomed to itself that it is blind to some of its own most dubious features. Levinas has two of them particularly in mind: abasement of humanity in the name of a less-than-transcendent God, and irresponsible acceptance, and even mystification, of suffering. Both deserve exploration.

Abasement of Humanity in the Name of a Less-Than-Transcendent God

To understand Levinas' contention with regard to the first feature, let us turn to two references in Levinas' text that can provide us with a clue to what he means. Levinas twice refers, with obviously *negative* connotations, to the Danish philosopher-theologian Søren Kierkegaard. Once he mentions him by name and characterizes his concept of faith as a *salto mortale*, a breathtaking acrobatic somersault—commonly known, in the English-speaking world, as "the leap of faith" [99-101]. A second time he refers to him by implication, by alluding to the title of one of his better-known works, *Fear and Trembling* [135].⁹ What is the point here?

Søren Kierkegaard (1813-1855) is considered by many as a precursor of the existentialist movement. A died-in-the-wool Romantic, Kierkegaard opposed two tendencies characteristic of early nineteenth-century philosophy of religion. The first was the tendency to think about *religion* in general (which in practice meant *ethical*) terms, in line with Kant's second critique. The second was the tendency to interpret Christian *doctrine* along *philosophical* lines, after the fashion of Hegel's systematic idealism. Kierkegaard viewed both trends as nothing less than characteristic instances of sinful presumption. God, he maintained, can be approached only in an attitude of complete personal surrender and awe, beyond all ethical or intellectual achievement. In that attitude of awe-struck surrender, *individual* human persons become most deeply conscious, in an acutely unsettling experience of "fear and trembling," that they are totally *inadequate before God*; yet at the same time they find themselves even more deeply and transparently *settled and rooted in God*, in faith.

For Kierkegaard, this experience of faith includes an essential element of salvation. For what is revealed to the person of faith is not only that humanity is inadequate before God. Rather, humanity is revealed as *desperate*: without faith, humanity is the unwitting victim of—to quote the title of another work by Kierkegaard—the true "sickness unto death": despair. Placed before God, human persons will realize that as long as they insist on thinking and acting on their own, all they will do is either desperately seek to maintain themselves (which is sin), or, unable to face themselves, desperately refuse to be themselves (which is sin). Only in the act of total abandon—

the dizzying feat of faith-surrender, the leap that defies all reason and all moral judgment—do people arrive at a true existence before God, which also assures them of salvation from sin and despair. Faith, in other words, is a deeply personal, "existential" risk freely though blindly taken, but a risk that is also rewardingly balanced by a deeply felt, deeply reassuring sense of God's presence, which, consequently, will transform all the elements of a person's life.

Levinas protests. In his eyes, it is "folly" to conceive of faith in terms of such "a direct contact with the Sacred, not based on reasonable grounds" [115-116]. Accordingly, he firmly rejects the corresponding experience of God's majesty "by way of palpable presence" [132; cf. 156-157]—"the felt experience of [God's] sacred mystery" [134-135].[10]

What is behind this protest? Levinas objects to this conception of faith because it is not appropriate for *adults*; it is *immature*. This deserves a careful historical explanation.

Ever since the theme of *redemption* became the center of the Christian faith (as in Anselm's *Cur Deus homo*), and certainly ever since Luther's desperate cry for a merciful God, and Melanchthon's firm reduction of the Gospel to the forgiveness of sins,[11] Western Christianity has tended to believe in God predominantly, and often exclusively, as *Savior*—a theme, moreover, that has tended to take on individualist overtones. But even apart from individualism, the development has tended to reduce the relationship between God and humanity to an opposition between human frailty and sinfulness and divine power and mercy.[12]

For all its devotionality, and indeed its relative truth, this view runs a dreadful risk. For what is thus placed at the heart of the Christian faith is not God's *kavôd*—the glory of God's transcendent majesty, nor the God-made glory of creation, nor the glory of humanity made in God's image and likeness, nor humanity's ineffable privilege of living in familiar partnership with God, nor humanity's vocation to be God's responsible representative in the world, but *wounded humanity's need for wholeness and redemption.* In this way, human weakness and sin, not human responsibility, move to the center of the faith-experience and tend to become the substance of history,[13] and humanity comes to cast itself in the role of the child, alternately requiring punishment and leniency. In this way, too, God's ability to meet the human need for redemption tends to become the measure of the divine greatness, and thus the transcendent

God is cast in the role of humanity's parent, sometimes stern, at other times indulgent.

All of this, Levinas contends, amounts to an attack, both on the transcendent majesty of God and on humanity's inalienable responsibility for a just world. There is infinitely more to God than God's being at the service of humanity's needs. A God mainly acknowledged as the Savior of humanity is no more than "a limited spirit" [50], "a rather elementary god" [47], and even "a strange magician" [50], who is the inhabitant of "the child's heaven" [60]. And if there is indeed such a thing as a "comforting sense of the divine presence," this can be no more than a provisional experience, for it is only "experienced in a *childlike* person's piety" [70-71].

These correlated conceptions of God and humanity, which Levinas rejects so vigorously as immature and provisional, have a natural side effect that is no less immature and provisional, and which Levinas both understands and rejects with equal vigor: *atheism*. If ability to meet human needs is taken to be the measure of God's omnipotence, then the apparent failure on God's part to constantly provide for human needs will eventually turn into a ground for the denial of God's existence.[14] Nothing, after all, is so volatile as the happiness of the immature. Wherever faith in God is expected to create, at the drop of a prayer, the presumption of a "warm, almost palpable communion with the divine," infantile disenchantment and fits of arrogance—peevish or heroic, as the case may be—are just around the corner in the form of "the desperate pride of the atheist" [156-158].

This type of immature faith, therefore, fails, and it does so on two counts.

First and most importantly, a God cast in the role of the omnipotent parent amounts to little more than a projection of basic human security-needs.

Such a conception is *unworthy of the living God*. Moreover (since experience teaches us that human needs for security are often unmet and human prayers for help are often unanswered) it leads straight into atheism, which, Levinas warns us, is no more than a "way station without God" on the road that leads from the children's God "to the one and only God" [57-58]—the God professed by the *Shema* (Deut 6, 4).

But secondly, this conception of faith is also *unworthy of humanity*, since it locks human beings into a stance of infantile dependency on divine comfort, and thus it fails to make room for "the full maturity of the integrally responsible person" [79-80], capable of action and endurance. It robs valiant people like Yossel Rakover of the privilege of "feel[ing], on his shoulders, all of God's responsibilities" [56-57]. It deprives them of the opportunity to consent, in the name of the living God, to being "victims [...] in a disordered world, that is to say, in a world where goodness does not succeed in being victorious" [76-78].

For these reasons, Levinas states, we are well rid of the magician-god. Incidentally, Levinas' rejection of this god is rather reminiscent of a theme developed by another victim of Nazi brutality, a Christian this time. I am referring to the theologian Dietrich Bonhoeffer, who rejected the "working-hypothesis" or "stop-gap" god that keeps humanity in tutelage and thus prevents it from coming of age.[15] For Bonhoeffer as for Levinas, the displacement of childish faith by atheism is a blessing in disguise. In fact, it is even a sign of growth: rejecting the magician-god is "the healthiest response" for all those who have been disabused of their faith "in a rather elementary god," who, fondly but foolishly, treats people "like perpetual children" [46-49].

At this point, however, Levinas goes one decisive step further. Judaism, he states, cultivates a mature form of faith—that is to say, a faith that does not depend on the experience of divine comfort, *and in this regard it is superior to Christianity*. For only a truly transcendent God can guarantee human maturity. Human maturity develops, not in an atmosphere of divine comfort or compassion, but whenever people realize they are being *done justice to* and taken seriously. Learning how to let oneself be taken seriously occurs by *training*; that is to say, by *teaching* and *discipline*—that is to say, by *Torah*, by the *Law*, given by the demanding, faraway, transcendent God: "The guarantee that there is a living God in our midst is precisely *a word of God that is not incarnate*" [105-107].

This is a highly significant expression. In Levinas' view, the immaturity of the Christian concept of God and humanity in their mutual relationship comes to a head in the Christian concept of *Incarnation*. Thus he explains that "the relationship between God and the human person is not *an emotional communion within the context of the love of an incarnate God*, but a relationship between minds that is mediated by teaching, by the Torah" [102-105]. Or, as he puts it elsewhere in the essay: "God is concrete, *not by means of incarnation*, but by means of the Law" [133-134]. He puts it even more strongly, and in more ominous tones, in a different essay, where he writes that, in the Christian faith, "the severe God who makes demands on a humanity capable of [doing] good is covered up by an infinitely indulgent deity who locks humans up in their wickedness and who delivers up to those humans, wicked yet saved, a defenseless humanity."[16] Seen in this light, God's infinite compassion with sinners, revealed in the Incarnation so ardently professed in Christianity, may in reality mask a God of radical injustice—a God who delivers an immature humanity up to its own evil in the very act of assuring it of indulgence, mercy, and love.[17]

This is a monstrous perspective. It is not only infantilizing, but highly neuroticizing, too.[18] For this frame of things capriciously and confusingly demands that one and the same God be feared as the judge who must condemn human wickedness, and loved for being an endlessly indulgent parent.

In opening up this perspective, Levinas calls into question the integrity of Christianity's central truth, the Incarnation. But that is not all. He also raises a second specter, in the form of the charge that Christianity, in an irresponsible fashion, accepts suffering and even mystifies it.

Irresponsible Acceptance and Mystification of Suffering

In his answer to the question "What is the meaning of the suffering of the innocent?" [42], Levinas shows that he is the heir of the great tradition encoded in the Scriptures of Israel. At bottom, what is at stake is one of Israel's perennial questions, brought to a head once again in an unprecedented fashion, in the near-extinction of the Jewish people in the Holocaust. That question is this: can we trust God to support justice in the world, which, after all, is God's own creation, professed to have been created "good" and indeed "very good" (Gen 1, 12. 18. 21. 25. 31)?

Biblical Israel always acknowledged that the Lord loves justice; from this, it had concluded that evildoers were bound to experience divine punishment, and experience it soon (Ps 37, 10. 35-36). It had also concluded that those who act justly were right in expecting to be divinely vindicated. This conception had enabled the prophetic tradition to interpret the contempt and oppression inflicted on Israel by a succession of historic enemies both as punishment for Israel's faithlessness and as an incitement to conversion, with a view to the restoration of Israel.

Still, there is an obvious evidentiary problem here: since evildoers do in fact very often prosper and have their way, where is the *evidence* for the proposition that the Lord hates evil? Bad things do happen to good people, and evil people get away with insolence and godlessness (Ps 73, 4-12). And if Israel, or Judah, ever recovered from the devastation of the Exile, it was only in the persons of the "little people" with no rights—the *'anawîm*. Thus both life experience and historical realism helped Israel unmask as naive any simple faith in the assured temporal rewards of the just life.

Ever more deeply, historic Israel entered into the realization that divine vindication is not regularly forthcoming, whether for the righteous individual or for the righteous nation. In time, sober wisdom quietly cultivated came to put an end to unrealistic assurance. In its place came a deeper, purer form of faith. Those who act justly, even if they are defeated by the violence of the powers that be, can take courage; if the violence does produce a crisis of faith in a just God (Ps 73, 2-14), this crisis is in reality a *test* of faith (cf. esp. the Book of Job). In this way, suffering and distress, in the mature experience of faith, become a sign of God's election: the just are justified in renewing and deepening their faith in God and in holding out, in long-suffering and perseverance. They are even justified in taking comfort from the hour of distress, in the assurance of God's certain, if hidden, judgment.

With the sure touch of the true believer, Levinas closes in on the passage in Kolitz' story that most fully embodies this great tradition, and provides it with a powerful commentary:

> [...] God withdraws himself from the world and veils his countenance. 'He has sacrificed humankind to its wild instincts,' says our text. '... And because those instincts dominate the world, it is natural that those who preserve the divine and the pure should be the first victims of this domination.'
>
> God veiling his countenance: I think this is neither a theologian's abstraction nor a poetic image. It is the hour when the just person has nowhere to go in the outside world; when no institution affords him protection; when even the comforting sense of the divine presence, experienced in a childlike person's piety, is withdrawn; when the only victory available to the individual lies in his conscience, which necessarily means: in suffering [61-73].

Unjust suffering, even the most senselessly unjust suffering, in this way becomes a sign of intimacy with God. In the Holocaust, those who are suffering the insane violence of the powers that be are doing so merely on account of their being Jews. Hence, the simple, "mindless" (*tout bêtement*) fact of being a Jew comes to mean intimacy with God:

> That is the intimacy that coincides, in one's conscience, with the pride of being Jewish, of being concretely, historically, altogether mindlessly, a part of the Jewish people. '[...] I am happy to belong to the unhappiest people in the world, to the people whose Torah represents the loftiest and most beautiful of all laws and moralities.'
>
> Intimacy with this virile God is attained in passing an ultimate test. Because I belong to the suffering Jewish people, the faraway God becomes *my God*. 'Now I know that you are truly my God, for you cannot possibly be the God of those whose deeds are the most horrible expression of a militant absence of God.' The just person's suffering for the sake of a justice that fails to triumph is concretely lived out in the form of Judaism. Israel —historical, carnal Israel—once again becomes a religious category [83-97].

Thus the meaning of the suffering of the innocent is: for them to know that they represent God in the world. But once this has been established, Levinas has one more point to make, to put Christians on notice. He writes:

> This is the specifically Jewish meaning of suffering—one that never takes on the quality of a mystical expiation for the sins of the world [73-75].

Levinas' reference is clear: Christians attribute to Christ's suffering, and to suffering undertaken in Christ's name, and often indeed to any suffering, an atoning, expiating significance; Jews do not. And in this regard, he implies, Jews are right, and Christians are wrong.

In Levinas' commentary on Zvi Kolitz' story, the text just quoted is the only one in which the Christian understanding of suffering as atoning is pointedly rejected. Hence, if we wish to understand more fully what Levinas means we will have to go to other passages in his work.

Two points have to be made. First of all, Levinas does emphati-

cally teach that human beings are meant to live in moral solidarity—
we are morally responsible to and for one another. In fact, it is one
of the fundamental elements of Levinas' thought that true, mature
human identity arises precisely out of the encounter with other
persons. It is precisely the defenseless faces of other persons looking
me in the eye that bring home to me the absolute demand that I
should let myself be "taken hostage" by them, that I should put
myself in their place ("substitution"[19]), in order thus to be in a position to do justice to them.[20] Hence,

> Among people, everyone is responsible for the mistakes of others.
> We are responsible even for the just person that runs the risk of
> corruption.[21]

But—and this is Levinas' second point—this *solidarity involves
no vicarious suffering* at all. In fact, Levinas objects to putting any
positive construction on vicarious suffering, on two counts. Firstly,
no victim's suffering can ever be alleviated by anyone else's suffering, or be taken over or cancelled by anyone else's suffering, let alone
be excused or justified by it. Secondly, those who inflict suffering
must never think of themselves as absolved—whether sacramen-
tally or in actuality—from the burden of moral responsibility they
must bear, simply because someone else has decided voluntarily to
absorb the violence they have caused:

> The personal responsibility of one person to another person is
> such that God cannot annul it. [...] an offense committed with
> regard to God is covered by the divine pardon, but an offense that
> affronts the human person is not covered by God. [... What must
> be affirmed is] the value and the full autonomy of the human
> person offended, as well as the responsibility incurred by anyone
> who touches the human person. Evil is not a mystical principle
> that can be wiped away by means of a ritual; it is an offense in-
> flicted by one person on another person. No one, not even God,
> can take the place of the victim. A world in which forgiveness is
> omnipotent becomes inhuman.[22]

Here we have finally come upon Levinas' real objection to the
Christian interpretation of suffering: it allows human beings to get
off the hook by dint of piety and sacrament. Christianity, Levinas
suggests, will bless people for shirking the moral responsibility that

is inalienably theirs. This will allow them to settle, in the name of God, for a less-than-human world in which innocent people are allowed to be put to the torture. In this way, Christians make God an accomplice in the injustice of the world. They tend to do so in two ways.

To the extent that Christians say that we live in a sinful world in which *evil is unavoidable,* they tend *to treat evil as excusable*: it is part of the human condition that people will sin, but this is meant to turn people to God's forgiveness, mercy, and love. In this way, a loving God becomes a theological excuse for moral irresponsibility. This will eventually make evil a matter of indifference. The German poet Heinrich Heine was uncomfortably close to this if indeed, on his death-bed in Paris in 1856, he both mocked and professed his faith in God when he quipped, "Of course he will forgive me; it is His trade."[23] Not surprisingly, the same Dietrich Bonhoeffer who rejected the stop-gap god that keeps humanity immature also rejected the average Christian's acceptance of divine mercy divorced from a commitment to conversion of life. This, he stated, amounted to a cheapening of God's grace as well as an approval of personal irresponsibility.[24]

To the extent that Christians acquiesce in the fact that this unavoidable *evil leads to suffering* on the part of innocent people, they tend *to mystify it*. That is to say, they tend to attenuate its full, scandalous reality either by presenting it as neutralized and depotentiated, in advance, by the vicarious suffering of Christ, or by affirming that it must be embraced on account of its mysterious redemptive power. Again, this amounts to an irresponsible tolerance of inhuman injustice in the name of a loving God.

No wonder that, in the Yiddish version of Kolitz' story, Yossel should come to a bitter conclusion: the merciful Christian God of Love has turned out to be far more life-threatening than the inexorable God who gave Israel its Torah. Paradoxically, reliance on the God of Love benevolently allows people to settle for complicity with cruelty and evil, whereas the demanding severity of the Torah, with its relentlessly jealous God, according to the Talmud, must be ever so leniently applied:

'Our God is a God of vengeance,' says Yossel ben Yossel, 'and our Torah is full of death penalties for venial sins. And yet it was enough for the Sanhedrin, the highest tribunal of our people in its land, to sentence a person to death once in seventy years to have the judges considered murderers. On the other hand, the God of the Gentiles has commanded to love every creature made in his image, and in his name our blood has been poured out for almost two thousand years' [121-129; *Yossel Rakover's Appeal to God*, expansion at line 135].

Judaism: An Integral Humanism Coupled with Difficult Worship

And so at last we come to the title of Levinas' essay. There is a final feature to Judaism, dreadfully underrated, in Levinas' view, by Christianity. In the Christian understanding of things, he suggests, the love of God—so forcefully commanded by the *Shema*—has been cheapened. In Levinas' eyes, therefore, loving God and being loved by God are suspect, because they can be so easily invoked in a self-serving manner. A religion that lives so much by divine love, he intimates, is bound to reduce God to a soft redemptive comforter who lets a pampered humanity get away with murder. So, he says, lest faith in the indulgent love of God dispense us from justice, from moral responsibility, let us love the stern demands of God's law—the Torah—more than God. And lest the glorious Name of God be tarnished by our childish fiduciality, let us do justice to God's greatness by standing before God as God invites us to stand: erect, in the posture of partners. For it is an insult to God as well as to humanity to define ourselves by our weakness and sinfulness and to grovel before God in the posture of the supplicant who can always fall back on a plea of ineptitude and beg for mercy. Here, Levinas says, lies the glory of Judaism. It realizes the presence of injustice in the world, but it does so in a way that does not relieve us from the duty to be deeply concerned about truly just, truly human institutions, in the name of a God who inexorably calls upon humanity to grow up, take charge of creation, and take responsibility for a just world.

It is also on this note that Levinas' essay ends. It is true, he writes, God is so immeasurably great that humankind is indeed totally incommensurate with God. But precisely because God is so immeasurably great, God does not, to be truly acknowledged as God, need a humanity riddled by inadequacy as a foil. From the fire that spells the infinite qualitative difference between God and us, God freely invites us to responsible partnership in the Covenant. For God is known as holy and wise and good, *not* because we—by contrast—are sinful, foolish, and evil, but because we, made in the divine image, are meant to be holy and wise and good, and capable of it. God desires human partners capable of *both* worshiping the divine glory *and* revealing it in history, not sinners, incompetents, dependents, and children, who take advantage of the divine mercy. And most of all, God does not want a humanity cut down to size and kept in its place by suffering and death—a humanity whose worship consists in crawling to the throne of grace. For the Name of God is the Lord, not Moloch.

These are formidable challenges. They come to Christianity from a Judaism that is independent and proud of a tradition that is as rooted in the Hebrew Scriptures as Christianity itself is. They must not be ignored. In the third section, therefore, we must raise the question whether the Christian faith deals with them, and if so how.

THREE

God's Love and God's Law

Preliminaries

Asymmetry and Creative Tension

In the introduction of this book, I promised that I would make some theological suggestions in this third section.[1] My *final* goal in presenting the arguments contained in this book, I stated, was *theological*, and I intended to offer a reinterpretation of the ancient Christian conviction about the fundamental asymmetry in the relationship between Christians and Jews. I promised that I would offer that reinterpretation to Christians first, but also to Jews, and not for acceptance but for examination and reflection.[2] The time has come to make good on these promises.

Before explaining and arguing the proposed reinterpretation in detail, let us briefly state it, in two points.

First of all, surprisingly perhaps, let me firmly state that I will not consign the idea of the asymmetry between Christianity and Judaism to the trash can where the great historic prejudices belong. On the face of it, a radical rejection of the whole idea of asymmetry might appear to be an attractive act of tolerance and broad-mindedness, not in the least because it would also acknowledge the fact that our several religious traditions have *de facto* gone their separate ways. But we must be careful. Rarely is it wise to consign important episodes in the past to oblivion and let bygones be bygones. It is often better, in the long run, to retrieve the uncomfortable past and face it and untangle it anew.

The fact is that the Christian faith remains irreversibly rooted in first-century Judaism and the Traditions it recognized. And no matter how unaware modern Christians may be, either of their roots in first-century Judaism or of historic Judaism as it has developed as a separate religious tradition, the Christian faith simply cannot exist or be itself if it allows itself to be cut loose from the faith of Israel. *Historically as well as theologically speaking*, what Ignatius of Antioch wrote is correct: "It was not Christianity that came to believe in Judaism, but Judaism in Christianity"[3]—even though, of course, it must be added at once that not all of Judaism came to believe in Christianity, nor even most of it. But in any case, awkward as it may appear at first blush, I propose to hold on to the asymmetry concept.

However, having stated this, let us immediately make a second point. The Christian affirmation of the asymmetry between Christianity and Judaism does not at all warrant the conclusion that Christianity has supplanted Judaism, *not even from a Christian point of view*. This is an important observation, so let us rephrase it for emphasis. It is indeed impossible to remove from Christianity, from its oldest scriptural layers on up, the conviction that Jesus Christ and the Christian faith to which he gave rise are the fulfillment of the faith and the expectations of Israel.[4] Both as a Christian and as a Catholic theologian I continue to accept that. Still, it is my contention that this acceptance does not at all commit us to the thesis that the Christian faith has displaced Judaism or dated it, *not even for Christians themselves.*

What I wish to propose, in other words, is that *from the point of view of Christian faith and theology* the peremptory characterization of Judaism as "fulfilled" in the sense of "displaced and dated"—a characterization unfortunately found with some frequency in the Church Fathers—is wrong. There is indeed a sense in which Judaism may be said to be fulfilled, but "fulfilled" may never come be understood as "dismissed."

Moreover I wish to argue, paradoxically, that the professed *asymmetry* between Christianity and Judaism is far from odious. Rather, it demands of Christians an abiding acknowledgment of and respect for the living tradition of Judaism and even, in some sense, an active participation in it. This is not just a matter of abstract ideas, but of both ideas and reality.

In other words, far from definitively encumbering the relationship between Judaism and Christianity with further mutual distrust and incomprehension, the asymmetry thesis, I wish to argue, places modern Jews and modern Christians in a *relationship of reciprocity*, which can, and should, also be a relationship of *dynamic tension*. Eventually, I will suggest that this dynamic tension between Christians and Jews is potentially creative. I will even venture further afield and argue that it is rooted in something Judaism and Christianity have in common: an eschatological faith-commitment, which in turn encompasses a commitment to peace and justice. And finally, in an effort (perhaps) to carry theological reflection to an extreme of buoyancy, I will even suggest that all of this may somehow already underlie the vigorous interest that so many Jews take in being involved, in a variety of ways, in such a deeply Christian and especially Catholic venture as a Catholic university.

As stated at the outset, I will argue these points as a Catholic theologian, and not as someone who is familiar with Judaism.[5] Yet the insights and arguments I will be proposing did come to me as a result of my efforts to understand and interpret the two modern Jewish texts read and interpreted in the previous two sections. The curious and liberating thing is that one may come to a purer, less cluttered understanding of the familiar in the very act of understanding and interpreting the unfamiliar. Prejudice blinds us, not only to others but also to our deeper selves. Analogously, in the very act of venturing beyond our own horizon, in our attempts to understand others, we find enlightenment for ourselves.

Hence, though these theological reflections are offered to fellow Christians first of all, for their examination and reflection, what I have to say may be illuminating to Jews, too, as they come to share the insights a Christian has gained for himself from the study of some of their heritage.

I shall develop my arguments under three principal headings, all of them touched on in the previous two sections. In light of Kolitz' story and Levinas' commentary, we will start with an analysis of *the Christian concept of Incarnation* so powerfully criticized by Levinas. It will be argued that, far from displacing the mature discipline of the Torah, as Levinas suggests, it actually confirms and even completes it.

Then, in a long second section, it will be explained that *the Christian claim that Christ is the fulfillment of the promises made to Israel does not mean that salvation is fully accomplished*, which would imply that Judaism could be said to have served its turn. In this context, a crucial distinction will be made: belief in the Incarnation involves the acceptance of Jesus Christ as the *representative* of humanity, not as its *substitute*. Consequently, far from letting Christians off the hook, faith in the Incarnation involves a commitment to responsibility in the pursuit of justice, which includes a commitment to the struggle on behalf of all those suffering unjustly anywhere.

Finally, in the third part of this section, I will argue that the Catholic Tradition agrees with Levinas in thinking of the religious life as "an integral and austere humanism, coupled with difficult worship! And from the other point of view, a worship that coincides with the exaltation of Man!"[6] This, I will suggest, provides a firm basis for Jewish-Christian collaboration, as well as one that is intellectually and theologically responsible.

1.   Torah and Incarnation

Incarnation and Resurrection

That Jesus Christ is God's Son, the Beloved (Mk 1, 11; 9, 7; parr Mt 3, 17; 17, 5; Lk 3, 22; 9, 35; Eph 1, 6; Col 1, 13), and the Word of God made flesh (cf. esp. Jn 1, 14) are core formulas of the Christian profession of faith. That profession of faith in Jesus' divine identity is immediately rooted in the revelation, by God, of Jesus as risen from the dead.[7] Jesus Christ risen from the dead on the third day and alive for God forever in the Holy Spirit is, therefore, the linchpin of the Christian faith. Apart from it, the Christian faith is meaningless (cf. 1 Cor 15, 17).

"Resurrection," we must recall first of all, is a metaphor, not of Christian, but of Jewish origin. In the idiom of first-century Judaism, it had a very specific meaning. It was a piece of Pharisaic spirituality, rejected by the Sadducee establishment that was connected with the Temple (cf. Acts 23, 6ff.; Mt 22, 23). "Resurrection" summed up the *confident hope*, held on to amidst oppression and injustice, that *final justice, for Israel as well as for the world,* was to be expected from God alone.[8] On the Lord's own Day, God's true servants were to be "revealed," "raised up," and "glorified": all those good people who had suffered violence at the hands of the powers that be for refusing to make common cause with injustice.

Both Jesus and his disciples were Jews, and not connected with the Temple establishment. Not surprisingly, therefore, God's revelation of Jesus alive, "vindicated in the Spirit" (1 Tim 3, 16), activated the Jewish resurrection metaphor. At the same time, at the hands of the first Christians, the metaphor acquired a prominence which it did not have in its original late-Jewish context.

What did the profession of Jesus risen involve? By raising him from the dead, the first Christians said, God, *and God alone,* had *vindicated Jesus,* condemned by the Jewish authorities as a scandalous blasphemer and executed by the Romans as a threat to the emperor's sacred authority. Thus God had revealed him as "the Holy and Just One" (Acts 3, 14). The profession that Jesus was risen, in other words, involved not only the affirmation of his divine identity, but also the acknowledgment of the holiness of his life. Consequently, Jesus' identification as God's Son went hand in hand with the recognition, in retrospect, of God's presence in his human life and death. What had been a matter of well-attested (Acts 2, 22; 10, 36ff.) *human* history now proved to have been *God's work*. If Jesus had "gone about doing good," this was because "God was with him" (Acts 10, 38). God had been mysteriously active even in Jesus' death: in God's mysterious design, the Christ had "had to" suffer to come into his glory (cf. Lk 24, 26).

For the first disciples, all of this meant that *God had begun to establish definitive justice* on earth. Hence their faith in Jesus risen also involved his identification as *the anticipated agent of God's final judgment*: "God has fixed a day on which he will do justice to the whole world by someone he has appointed, and he has guaranteed this to all by raising him from the dead" (Acts 17, 31). This, far from being a message of pure comfort and assurance, implied a call to repentance and conversion. A different way of conveying the same idea was the affirmation that Jesus had been revealed as the standard by which God would judge: the way people acknowledged him was going to determine the way God would acknowledge them (cf. Mt 10, 32-33). Again, this implied not just assurance but also a warning. It is not enough to acknowledge Jesus as Lord; what is called for is doing the will of the God whom Jesus had called *Abba*—his "dear Father" (Mt 7, 21 coll. Lk 6, 46). The Christian identification of Jesus as God's Son, therefore, sets standards for action.

Jesus and Torah

Very concretely, this meant that both Jesus' life and his person became for the Christian community the key to a new, and indeed definitive, reading of the Scriptures—above all of the Torah. That is to say, the Scriptures and Jesus' person and life became *mutually illuminating*. The Scriptures of Israel, for their part, authoritatively interpreted Jesus and all he stood for. And conversely, Jesus' person and life, now appreciated in the retrospect inspired by the Resurrection, enabled the Christian communities to interpret the Scriptures in a new, authoritative manner.[9] The New Testament orchestrates the theme in a variety of ways, too many to elaborate here. A few suggestions must suffice.

The theme is very clear, for example, in the Gospel of Matthew. That gospel, so full of references to the fulfillment of the Scriptures, insists that, despite conflicts with certain religious authorities on the interpretation of specific points in the Torah, Jesus clearly considered it his mission not to abolish it, but to see it lived out to perfection. Characteristically, Matthew's gospel also preserves Jesus' words in the form of five large discourses reminiscent of the five books of Moses, and thus by implication casts Jesus in the role of the giver of the new law.[10]

An important way in which the early Christian communities came to express their faith in Jesus as Messiah and Lord derives from contemporary Jewish *wisdom traditions*. The cultivation of wisdom had long been an interest common to many cultures of the Ancient Near East. In Israel, the genre was traditionally connected with the figure of Solomon, as legendary for his wisdom in governance (cf. 1 Kings 3, 5-14; Prov 1, 1; 10, 1; 25, 1) as for his cosmopolitan outlook. After the Exile, the cultivation of wisdom yielded such collections of traditional moral and religious instruction as the Book of Proverbs, and such remarkable writings as Job, Sirach, and Qohelet, and, in the diaspora, the Wisdom of Solomon. As wisdom's relationship with God was further explored, it became personified and increasingly acquired divine features. In the diaspora, this Jewish theme found support in current Hellenistic thought (Wisd 7, 25ff.; 8, 3; 9, 4). Thus wisdom could come to be acknowledged as the pre-existent, heavenly original of the Torah, which in due course had found its proper dwelling place in Zion (Sir 24, 8-12). But on a more universalist note, this Wisdom came to be acknowledged as operative since the beginning of things: it had been God's own agent in creation (Prov 3, 19-20; 8, 22-31), the Word by which God had created the world (Sir 24, 3-4). In that capacity, Wisdom was thought of as omnipresent, at home "in every people and nation" (Sir 24, 7), even though it was believed to have come to dwell preeminently in Israel.

No wonder that the figure of Jesus, once risen, came to be definitively interpreted, by means of the stylistic device known as personification, as the preexistent divine Wisdom, equally at home with God and in the world. The theme is especially prominent in the Letter to the Hebrews (esp. Heb 1, 1-2), and in the prologue of the fourth Gospel, where it has strong affinities with *Logos*-speculations current in contemporary Hellenistic Judaism.[11] Thus, in a bold move, the Christian community began to claim on behalf of the historical person of Jesus what Judaism had come to claim on behalf of divine Wisdom. First of all, Jesus came to be acknowledged as the preexistent Torah Incarnate, the Word of divine Wisdom made flesh, dwelling among those who had welcomed him and thus had gotten empowered to become God's children (cf. Jn 1, 12. 14). But secondly, in a more universalist vein, Jesus, the Word of God, came to be acknowledged as the key to the very existence and coherence of the world as a whole (cf. Jn 1, 2-3; Col 1, 16)—a theme the second-century Christian apologists were to pursue with special vigor.

Preexistence christology (nowadays often referred to as "descent-christology" or "christology from above") was not the only fruit of the Christian familiarity with Jewish wisdom literature. We must look at another, equally striking example of the way in which Christian communities availed themselves of wisdom traditions to profess their faith in Jesus as Son of God. Anticipating the "ascent-christologies" (or the "christologies from below") of a later day, they depicted Jesus, especially in his passion, as the exemplar of obedient fidelity to God in the face of unjust persecution.

Jesus' Suffering in Fidelity to God

In the Septuagint, the authoritative Greek version of the Scriptures that was widely used in the Jewish diaspora, in the deuterocanonical (or "apocryphal") book known as Wisdom of Solomon, there occurs a passage that bears quoting in full. The passage purports to be a sample of the scornful talk of the impious (Wisd 2, 10-20):

> Let us tyrannize the righteous poor person;
>> let us not spare the widow,
>>> nor respect the white hairs of the elderly.
> But let our power be the norm of what is just,
>> for whatever is weak is obviously useless.
> Let us entrap the just person,
>> for he is inconvenient to us,
>> and he opposes our actions,
>> and he reproaches us for violating the Law,
>> and he denounces us for violating our upbringing.

He claims to have knowledge of God,
    and calls himself a child of the Lord.
He has become for us an indictment of our designs;
    the very sight of him is a burden to us,
For his style of life is unlike that of others,
    and his ways are entirely different.
We are considered frauds by him,
    and he keeps his distance from our ways as if they were
        unclean;
    he calls the last end of the just blessed,
    and boastfully claims God for his Father.
Let us see if his words are true,
    and let us try out what will happen when he comes to his
        end.
For if the just person is the Son of God,
    God will take care of him,
    and save him from the power of his opponents.
Let us put him on trial by insolence and torture,
    so that we may find out how accommodating he is,
    and let us put his long-suffering to the test.
Let us sentence him to a disgraceful death,
    for from what he says, he will be protected.

This is a classic picture of the dynamics of violence by which just persons will be subjected to undeserved suffering at the hands of the violent, *on no grounds other than the just lives they lead.* The passage reminds us that we would fail to fathom the mystery of human sin if we were to think of it merely in terms of weakness in the face of temptation or overreaction to the sins of others. It must not be overlooked that there is an element of unholy willfulness and spontaneity in human sin: *the mere encounter with honest virtue will often suffice to provoke the human penchant for violence.* This is a measure of the deep-seatedness of sin: it can be elicited by virtue. We apparently take ordinary goodness to be so implausible that encountering it whets a perverse appetite for verification in us. There must be a way, we tend to feel, to lay bare the sinfulness even of the apparently innocent among us and to trigger the hidden springs of violence in them, too. Thus the sinful will not rest until they have tested the just and proved, in the interest of their own self-justification, that the just are only seemingly innocent and that they are in reality everybody's accomplices in sinfulness.

But what about those among us who succeed in resisting the temptation to join the violent in their efforts to put the just to the test? Many of us tend to stand by idly and impotently as the violent throw their weight around to test the virtuous. Does this not make guilty bystanders of us and demonstrate that we have at least some deep-seated doubts about the value of the innocence of others?

In such a situation, where ultimately can the just person turn for vindication, except to God—a God who, given the pervasiveness of violence, can only be experienced as the God who is, in the final analysis, hidden? Only the truly wise person's vision will enter into the mystery of this hidden God: in suffering without cause, the just know that they are ultimately being tested by God, and in that testing being found worthy of God (cf. Wisd 3, 5).

The passage from the Book of Wisdom just quoted undoubtedly represents, directly or indirectly, one of the principal sources of the synoptic narratives of Jesus' Passion. In using the passage as a model, the gospels, especially Matthew, avail themselves of the Jewish wisdom tradition to cast Jesus in the role of the person who has irritated the powers that be and is now being unjustly persecuted by them. Apparently abandoned by God, he becomes the complete victim of the human determination to test his faith in God. Taunted to save himself or at least to get himself saved by the invisible God who has become his sole trust and his sole resort, he accepts death rather than compromise his fidelity to God. In this way, his very suffering becomes the proof both of his faith and of the integrity of his justice.[12] In much the same tradition, the gospel of Mark presents Jesus' manner of dying as evidence of his divine sonship by having the Roman centurion who has headed the execution squad profess it: "When the centurion, who stood there facing him saw that he had thus breathed his last, he said, 'Truly that man was God's Son'" (Mk 15, 39). With a variation of Yossel Rakover's words we could say that, if it could ever be doubted that God had designated Jesus as the chosen one, it can be believed that his tribulations have made him the chosen one.[13]

At this point we can broaden the discussion. By now it should be clear why it is possible to establish such a striking similarity between Zvi Kolitz' figure of Yossel Rakover and the suffering Jesus of Nazareth of the synoptic gospels: the wisdom tradition used by the gospel to interpret the figure of the suffering Jesus is exactly the same as the tradition used by Kolitz to interpret, not just the faith of the Jews in the midst of suffering, but the very essence of what it means to be a Jew, as Levinas well saw.[14]

One of the more sophisticated writings of the New Testament, the Letter to the Hebrews, shows the same pattern. That letter is one sustained exhortation to disciplined perseverance in the faith, in imitation of Jesus, who remained faithful to God, and who has now, in his risen state, entered the heavenly sanctuary, from where he encourages the faithful to endure in their faith-commitment. But remarkably, for all his sovereignty, Jesus is not presented as unaffected by distress and suffering. In fact, the opposite is true. Jesus' fidelity to God is depicted as a matter of *obedience* practiced in the teeth of *temptation; tested faith* identifies him as the saving Son of God (Heb 2, 14-18; 4, 14-15; 5, 7-10; 12, 2-3). Nor does Jesus occupy this place of honor as if he were a paragon of solitary perfection. No, he sums up and crowns a *tradition*. That tradition turns out to be *Israel's* great tradition of tested faith in an invisible God who made the world and who holds out hope for everlasting goods (cf. Heb 11, 1-3). For that reason, the Letter to the Hebrews can enumerate Abel, Enoch, Noah, Abraham, Sarah, Isaac, Jacob, Joseph, Moses, Rahab the harlot, Gideon, Barak, Samson, Jephtha, David, Samuel and the prophets, as well as the martyrs of the later Jewish struggles for freedom. All of them are presented as "attested by their faith": they kept on believing even though they did not see God's promise come true (cf. Heb 11, 4-39).[15]

Conclusions

It is possible to draw two conclusions from the preceding series of arguments. Both Zvi Kolitz and Marc Chagall raise the question whether the suffering Jesus can be, or must be, recognized as the associate of suffering Jewry.[16] To this question the answer must be, *on scriptural grounds*, an unqualified yes. And what must be immediately added is, of course, that the tradition of Jewish faith tested by suffering, of which (Christians say) Jesus is the high point, did not die out with the birth of the Christian Church. Jesus, therefore, must also be recognized as the associate of all Jews that have unjustly suffered in the course of the Christian Era.

Secondly, Christians must learn anew that Jesus' suffering *as a faithful Jew* is precisely one of the meanings of what later Christian doctrine came to call the Incarnation. "The Word became flesh" and "Jesus is the Son of God, the Chosen One" mean that Jesus embodies and personifies to perfection Israel's Torah, the Wisdom of God, faithfully and obediently lived out "in a disordered world, that is to say, in a world where goodness does not succeed in being victorious."[17]

It has already been pointed out that the identification of Jesus as the Word Incarnate and as the Chosen Son of God comes to the Church in the light of the Resurrection, which is the revelation of God's judgment that Jesus is the Holy and Just One (Acts 3, 14).[18] Hence, it is thanks to the Resurrection that Jesus is proclaimed as having fulfilled the Torah and all the divine promises held out in it.

This observation leads to the second series of arguments. It remains to be shown that belief in Jesus Christ as God Incarnate does not commit the Christian to the thesis that salvation is complete, and hence, that Judaism, along with its hopes for salvation, is definitively displaced. An important consequence of this, it will be argued, is the acceptance of Jesus Christ as the *representative* of humanity, not as its *substitute*.

2. The Incompleteness of Salvation

Christ's Resurrection and the Disciplined Life

It is the central Christian conviction that Jesus has fulfilled the Torah and all of God's promises held out in it, on two counts. That Jesus has fulfilled the Torah is, first of all, implied in his Resurrection: Christians believe that Jesus has been revealed by God as risen and as Son of God, and thus as the fulfillment of the Torah in person. Secondly, Jesus' life and suffering in total fidelity to God, too, is to be understood as the fulfillment of the Torah. The problem is that there is a tendency in Christianity to exaggerate this conviction. The gist of the exaggeration is to equate faith in Jesus Christ as the fulfillment of the Torah with faith in *the completeness of salvation*. This amounts to a dangerous misinterpretation of Christian belief—one which, among other things, jeopardizes Christianity's relationship with Judaism.

Neither the faith nor the memories of the early Christian communities suggest that Jesus' Resurrection, and hence, his revelation as the Son of God Incarnate, meant that salvation was complete.[19] In the Christian *missionary proclamation* to Jews as well as Gentiles, the preaching of Christ became a call to conversion, in anticipation of God's judgment, to be revealed in due time in Christ's coming in glory (cf., e. g., 1 Thess 1, 9-10; Acts 10, 34-43; 17, 30-31). *Within the Christian communities*, the worshipful profession of Jesus as Lord was seen as a first, incipient participation in Jesus' glory, by the gift of the Holy Spirit. Hence, if Christians considered themselves saved (or, in Pauline language, "justified") in this way, they also knew that they were still awaiting the complete fulfillment of the promises, and hence, they knew they were to ready themselves, in watchfulness and prayer, for their definitive participation in Christ's risen life with God.

It must be pointed out, therefore, with all possible emphasis, that the Christian reinterpretation of Jewish eschatology amounted not to its abolition but—if anything—to its sharpening. To put this differently: the fundamental asymmetry between Judaism and Christianity is based on the conviction that the Law and all God's promises have been fulfilled *in Jesus*, now that he "has risen as the first-fruits of those who have died" (1 Cor 15, 20; cf. 23). But for the rest, the harvest remains to be brought in: *the Christian Church* continues to aspire, *like Judaism*, to the fullness of salvation. In fact, the very acknowledgment that Jesus has attained the total fulfillment of the promises of salvation serves to put in vivid relief the fact that the Christian community has not.[20]

One telling way in which the New Testament shows its awareness of this can be found in its treatment of the Law and of the figure of Moses behind it. In the Christian communities, the commitment to the strict observance of the Mosaic law was indeed replaced by faith in Jesus Christ; but this did not mean that Christians had simply left all Law behind. They had received *a new mediator* and hence, *a new and deeper source of faith-assurance*, in the person of Jesus the Son of God, in whom they had received an unprecedented access to God (cf., e.g., 2 Cor 3, 4 - 4, 6), essentially superior to what they came to see as the mediated access afforded by the Law (Gal 3, 19; Acts 7, 38. 53; Heb 2, 2). Still, far from interpreting this deeper assurance simply as divine indulgence, they realized that it also put them under a new obligation. That is to say, it put them more keenly at risk (cf., e.g., 1 Cor 10, 1-22; Heb 10, 19-31; 12, 18-29). Thus, far from being allowed to interpret their freedom from the Mosaic law as an easement, they got a far more demanding law to obey, which the emancipation from the full rigor of the Mosaic Law had imposed on them: the call to serve, not themselves, but others (cf. Gal 5, 13; Jas 1, 25; 1 Pet 2, 16; cf. 1 Cor 8, 9; 9, 19; cf. also Mk 10, 45).

Not surprisingly, therefore, when they set about fleshing out the demands of that new law, they went back to universalist Judaism, and specifically to the Book of Wisdom, according to which "love of [divine] Wisdom" leads to "desire for instruction" and "keeping of the laws" and *vice versa* (Wisd 6, 17-18). Christians, in other words, kept appealing to the Jewish Scriptures to lend authority to the more universalist rules of conduct they began to develop for themselves.[21]

It is clear, therefore, that Christians did not take cover behind the idea of divine love. Faith in Jesus did introduce Christians more deeply to the unfathomable mystery of God's love (Rom 5, 8; 1 Jn 4, 10), which demanded an unqualified love of neighbor. The most

distinctive feature of this love as enjoined on the Christian community, now composed of Jews as well as Gentiles, was that it involved
an extension of the neighborly love enjoined by the Torah (Lev 19,
18). Christian love was henceforth to include outsiders, on a basis of
equality (especially within the household of the faith: Gal 6, 10). But
that wider love was invariably seen as the fulfillment and the principle of coherence of the Law, not its abolition (Rom 13, 8. 10; Mt 22,
39-40; Gal 5, 14). In fact, the love command is codified again: it is
concretized by means of exhortations to practice very specific vir-
tues and to avoid very specific vices (cf., e. g., Col 3, 1-15).[22] There is
nothing in the New Testament to suggest that the Christian claim to
fulfillment implies contempt of *training, discipline,* (cf., e. g., 1 Cor 11,
32; Eph 6, 4; 2 Tim 3, 16; Heb 12, 3-11), or *teaching*—that is to say, *Law.*

Thus Paul, in his determination to present faith, not works, as
the basis upon which people are saved, will insist that it is on account
of *faith* that God, who is the One God of Jews and Gentiles, will justify
both those who are committed, by circumcision, to the works of the
Law and those not so committed; and he will immediately add that
in saying this he is upholding the Law (Rom 3, 29-31).

In the same way, nowhere in the various traditions in the New
Testament is it glossed over that Christians consider Jesus essentially superior to Moses (2 Cor 3, 7-18; Jn 1, 17-18; cf. 9, 27-33; Heb 3,
2-6); *in that sense,* the order of the Torah has been definitively out-
shone. But in the end, in the heavenly Jerusalem of the Apocalypse,
there is only one song to worship the one God, sung by those who
have conquered the beast: "the song of Moses, the servant of God,
and the song of the Lamb" (Rev 15, 3). In the final, all-encompassing praise of God offered by the redeemed, the Law is remembered,
not forgotten. [23]

A Serious Question

All of this raises a question. If what has been explained so far is true,
where did a responsible thinker like Levinas get the idea that Christianity has displaced the God of mature faith with a children's God,
and undermined the human responsibility to do justice by assuring
humanity of God's infinite mercy, thus introducing the element of
moral irresponsibility which he views as integral to the Christian
faith?

The answer to that question must be found in history, in certain historical developments within Christianity that must in all frankness be called dubious, both because of what they did to distort the Christian faith and on account of the way they influenced Jewish-Christian relationships. Those developments, incidentally, account not only for what Levinas sees as elements of injustice and immaturity in the Christian faith, but also for the misunderstanding of what I have called the asymmetry between Judaism and Christianity.

It is, of course, impossible to give a complete treatment of this issue here. Still, three important and interconnected developments must be enumerated and briefly elaborated.

Christianity as the Roman Empire's Established Religion

First of all, we must recall a fact that was to determine the shape of the Christian Church in the West for twelve centuries, if not longer: in the course of the fourth century, the Christian Church became the state religion of the Roman empire.

What took place was roughly this. Since the first generation of Christians, as the New Testament writings show, the Resurrection of Jesus had been interpreted as God's eschatological victory over sin, death, and the powers that be, and hence, as the firstfruits—the beginning of the harvest of the new creation (1 Cor 15, 20. 23). In such a framework, those who had, in the footsteps of Christ the Lamb, patiently endured persecution for their faith and died in it could also be called the firstfruits of God's new creation (Rev 14, 4). Even those who had been reborn by the message and were living it out in patience could be called "in some sense the firstfruits [*aparchēn tina*] of God's creation" (Jas 1, 18). But one thing was clear: God's harvest remained to be brought in. For all its assurance of salvation, Christianity's theme was hope, not attainment; the present was marked by provisionality, not permanence. The Christian life was a life of expectancy, not establishment.

When, however, the emperor Constantine attributed his victory over his rival Maxentius at the Milvian bridge in C.E. 312 to the Cross of Christ, a marked shift of perspective began to take place. Constantine granted the Church civil recognition. This in turn came to be interpreted as a public sign of God's endorsement of the Christian faith, and as the visible part of Christ's eschatological triumph. In this way, redemption could come to be presented as a *fait accompli*, as a stable state of salvation given *in the public structures of the Church as such*. The gradual adoption of imperial ceremony to glorify liturgically the cross of Christ as the Church's victory banner, and the bestowal of senatorial rank on the Church's leadership were but a few of the many ways in which the Church acquired features that caused it to be less than entirely mindful of its pilgrim state. With the visible Church so prominently established, the Kingdom of God—still unaccomplished—tended to move into the background. With the redemptive work of Christ looking so complete, what was more or less lost sight of was that the salvation of the world was still to be achieved.

It is true, the tendency was not universal. Augustine, for one, was not entirely sanguine about the establishment of the Church. He was realistic enough to remain aware of failure and sin in the Church and careful enough not to equate it with the City of God. But Eusebius, the author of a very influential, sweeping history of the world and the Church, had a vision that was all the more commanding for being so uncomplicated. So did many of his successors in Christian historiography.

At the end of the tenth book of his *Ecclesiastical History*, after describing how Constantine defeated his rival Licinius, Eusebius casts the Emperor Constantine in the role of the divinely appointed agent. He restores the ancient *pax romana*, in the form of the perfect state this time: the all-encompassing Christian Kingdom, the culmination and end of history. As a modern student of Eusebius puts it, "All humankind had been bound up into the cosmic liturgy, singing continuous hymns to God while the good emperor, the Friend of God, rules with *philanthrōpia* and *eusebeia*."[24]

Thus there developed a new situation: the ancient state religion of Rome was gradually replaced by a triumphant, or at least established, Christian Church, which did not always resist the temptation to blur the distinction between earth and heaven. This became even more true when both pagans and heretics were outlawed by imperial decree (Theodosius' *Cunctos populos*, C.E. 380). Needless to say, in such a situation, Jews, being neither pagans nor heretics, could hardly feel at home.

All of this profoundly affected the Church's understanding of its relationship to Judaism. The second-century marginalization of the Jewish-Christian communities, evident, for example, in the writings of Irenaeus of Lyons, had already caused an appreciable loss of contact with Judaism as a living tradition. The fourth-century Constantinian establishment now favored a much deeper alienation. In the context of the Church's establishment as the state religion, the Christian interpretation of Christ and his Church in terms of the fulfillment of God's promises made to Israel could far more easily degenerate into a theology in which fulfillment came to mean displacement. The Christian claims were, of course, bound to look more questionable. As the Church got more aligned with the political realities of the empire, it was forced to settle for a certain amount of institutional injustice as part of life; political alliances always involve a certain amount of complicity. Consequently, the claim of the imperially protected Christian Church to represent the fulfillment could never be sufficiently backed up by a commitment to justice and holiness consistent enough to sound entirely credible.

In such a context, a dreadful development was only too close at hand. If the truth of the Christian faith had been divinely vindicated in the displacement of paganism and in the Constantinian establishment, how to account for the continuing Jewish diaspora—Judaism's obvious disestablishment—except as a palpable sign of divine punishment and rejection? Punishment and rejection for what? The answer had to be ominously clear: the Jews had killed the Son of God. In the Constantinian establishment, the politico-theological warrants for the development of institutional anti-Semitism are not very far to seek. Displacement of Judaism by Christianity as a matter of right was more than likely to turn into discrimination of Jews in a Christian state as a matter of might. The invention of the legend of the wandering Jew became a matter of time.

Seen in this very long perspective, it is possible to appreciate the historic importance of the second Vatican Council's decision to put an end to any surviving traditions of displacement theology. The Council did so by going to the root of the problem: it recovered the classic conception of the Kingdom of God. God's Kingdom, the Council explained, is proposed in a variety of ways in the Scriptures of Israel, and "is manifested above all in the very Person of Christ," who made it the central focus of his preaching and ministry. Consequently, it must also be the life-giving principle of the Church. This conception entirely relates the Church to the Kingdom of God: the Church is its messenger and its agent, its seed and its beginning. At heart, the Church is nothing if not the yearning for the promised

Kingdom.[25]

These moves have many profound consequences, which are likely to take decades to come to fruition. In the present context, let me mention two. First of all, gone is the Catholic Church's apparent claim to represent salvation as fully achieved. Much as the Church has the promise of God's creative and merciful love as revealed in the risen Christ, the new heaven and the new earth are far from accomplished. For Christians, too, peace is a matter of hope not attainment, and Jerusalem a vision of peace not its accomplishment. Secondly, in this way the Catholic Church has regained the freedom to recognize that in acknowledging Jesus as the fulfillment of Israel, it need not in any way claim the Kingdom of God, or salvation, for itself alone. This in turn makes it also understandable why the Church should have come to call itself by a name that it shares with countless others—the name that was Israel's long before it was the Church's: "the People of God."

Dependency as a Prevalent Style of Faith

In due course, Christianity's position as the established state religion of the Roman Empire gave rise to a second development, which is as understandable as it is questionable: the development of a type of faith that is characterized by dependence on ecclesiastical assurance. This deserves an explanation.

No matter how committed to the idea of its holiness the ancient Church may have been, its awareness of failure and sin never faded: the praise of God for the salvation assured in Christ risen was always tempered by the prospect of judgment and hence by the Church's prayer for mercy. But failure and sin became an obvious as well as a very much tolerated reality in the Church when the Constantinian establishment was continued, after the collapse of the Roman Empire, into the early medieval period and far beyond. Over a span of roughly five centuries, as Europe became christianized, entire tribes were converted along with their chieftains, without, however, the deeper conversion that had been the rule in the ancient Church, even under the imperial aegis. But if everybody is a Christian, nobody is—or at least only relatively few. "Christendom" does not connote the same depth of faith as "Church." If Christendom had reason to be proud of its religious and cultural achievements, it is also undeniable that it had settled for an attenuated conception of the normative life of faith. As Baptism became almost a natural consequence of birth, it was also more and more interpreted in a passive sense, as the washing away of original sin, and less and less as a privilege and a vocation that involves a commitment to a shared life of holiness.

In this situation, as fewer and fewer of its members measured up to the demands of the Christian life in any demonstrable fashion, the Church began to appeal all the more strongly to the inherent holiness of its God-given institutions, especially the sacraments, whose *ex opere operato* efficacy came to be understood as *supplementing* and even *replacing* personal faith, rather than *grounding* it. Not surprisingly, the age-old sacramental catechesis that stressed the theme of *sharing in Christ's mystery* was more and more modified to suit the situation in which fewer and fewer Christians qualified for regular participation in the Church's sacramental celebrations. The new theme of sacramental catechesis, more pertinent to the real situation, was not *participation in*, but *reliance on*, Christ's mystery. That mystery had been entrusted to the Church in the form of the infinite treasury of merits gained by Christ's suffering and death on behalf of sinners. That treasury was to be reverently guarded and responsibly dispensed by the ordained officers in the Church, especially by offering Mass for the living and the dead.

No wonder that the Church, as it grew and developed in a feudal world, acquired feudal features. In a world in which the majority lived at the sufferance of a small minority of leaders—vicariously, as it were—the majority of Christians became believers in a dependent, vicarious fashion; they lived on ecclesiastical assurance. No wonder, either, that the clergy got more and more identified, by means of a whole, very coherent set of new idioms, as "the Church," whose essential task it was to dispense salvation to sinners.

It has often been pointed out that the growth and development of the medieval Church provide a striking example of the Church's apostolic compassion and service to the world. It is true, in recognizing and adapting to the very imperfect realities of medieval social and political life, the Christian Church was also remarkably successful in transforming them. And yet, there is also a dark side to this version of Christianity. It tolerated and institutionalized a very imperfect type of faith, marked by unacceptable compromises. In meeting the needs of the many, it also limited their faith to the passive acceptance of salvation. This amounted to an institutional diminishment of the fullness of Christian life on the part of the majority of the Church's membership. In doing so, Christendom settled for dependence, immaturity, and diminished responsibility on the part of the "simple faithful" as normal, and even as normative.[26]

Again, the Second Vatican Council has marked a historic move away from this situation. It has stressed that full membership in the Church belongs to all members of the Church in virtue of Baptism, and consequently, that all have a common vocation to holiness.[27]

Substitutionary Atonement

The cultivation of dependence as a widespread characteristic of Christian faith led to a dangerous doctrinal development. The origin of this development was quite legitimate: the New Testament affirmation that Jesus suffered and died *"for us."*[28] The problem was that the affirmation got so twisted that it came to mean something entirely alien to the New Testament.

The New Testament teaching, widely explained and developed by the Church Fathers, can be summarized as follows. In willingly suffering and dying, in complete obedience to God, Jesus had achieved what sinful humanity was incapable of achieving: reconciliation with God. This reconciliation was accomplished by Jesus' *representing* humanity. Though sinless, he had voluntarily, out of love and compassion, shared and taken responsibility for the sinful human predicament, down to accepting a criminal's death *at the hands of sinful people*. In doing so, Jesus had abandoned himself completely to God, and God had accepted his self-offering and raised him to life. In this way the whole work of salvation was ultimately rooted in the love of God, whose Son had taken on humanity, along with its inhumanity, in order to redirect it and renew it and bring it home to God. Communion with the risen Christ, therefore, means the restoration of true humanity: it *enables* all those who believe in him to live for God *and* for others again, in the knowledge that their sins are forgiven. Consequently, having been "redeemed dearly" (1 Cor 6, 20; cf. 1 Pet 1, 18-19), Christians are *"saved"*—that is, *restored to freedom before God* and *called to responsibility in following Jesus Christ in his love for others*, for the salvation of the world.

It is clear that this conception of Christ's saving work entails responsibilities for those who accept its benefits. Christ's suffering, death, and resurrection do not get anyone off the hook. No one one can rest in the assurance of a salvation procured, at great expense to himself, by someone else. On the contrary, saved by Christ, Christians are drawn into discipleship and called, in the words of Paul, to "spend and be spent" (2 Cor 12, 15). This is also the teaching of the great Christian Tradition: actively, the *"law of Christ"* calls for the active *shouldering of others' burdens* (Gal 6, 2) out of compassion; passively, God's blessing rests on the *patient, willing acceptance of undeserved suffering*, in imitation of Christ *the Lamb* (cf. Jn 1, 29; 1 Pet 1, 19; 2, 19-24; 3, 14; 4, 13-16; Mt 5, 10).

This classic Christian doctrine came to be miserably misrepresented, especially in popular preaching, in a late-medieval Church that was rightly preoccupied by a prevalence of institutional sin in its midst. In a glaring misreading both of the New Testament and of what Anselm of Canterbury had written in his *Cur Deus homo*, Jesus' death came to be interpreted as *divine punishment for human sin*.[29] God, in this construction, had angrily demanded *punishment in return for atonement*, and Jesus "had had to" be despatched, not as humanity's representative, but as humanity's *substitute*—that is to say, as its *scapegoat*. The problem is, of course, that the New Testament consistently teaches that Jesus suffered *in behalf* of humanity; it *never* says that he suffered *"instead* of us."

The enormous difference between these two expressions can be clarified by distinguishing between *representation* and *substitution*.[30] Someone who *represents* me does not *replace* me: I remain involved— there remains an active relationship of mutual responsiveness, which implies a continuing responsibility on my part. Someone who is my substitute, however, supplants me, displaces me, excludes me, makes me superfluous. In other words, whereas *representation invites participation, substitution excludes it*.[31] *A Jesus viewed as humanity's representative involves us*: he acts on our behalf in such a way as to restore us to our relationship with God and to our responsibility for humanity and the world. *A Jesus viewed as humanity's substitute excludes us*: he settles the debt humanity owes to God by exempting everyone from what *he* did and suffered. Such a Jesus absolves us from our responsibilities for each other and for the world.

In this latter construction, the world is redeemed by a purely heavenly transaction between God and Jesus Christ—one that occurred without our involvement and from which we benefit without our assent. This type of salvation is humanly unacceptable; it is unworthy of mature, responsible humanity.

If the human implications of this construction are unacceptable, the theological implications are positively appalling. A Jesus viewed as a substitute for humanity reveals a God who, like an omnipotent ruler who owes no one an explanation and who shows his power by being capricious, has decided, his anger appeased by the suffering and death of Christ, to impute his "merits" to humanity free of charge. This makes the suffering and death of an innocent human being into a punishment for sin darkly and ominously willed by a mortally offended God, yet also, at the same time, into the saving expedient, mysteriously effective for the salvation of the world, by an inscrutable divine design. Confusingly, the one God must in the same act be feared as the judge who, in cold blood, demands whatever he decides he wants in the way of satisfaction for human wickedness, and loved for being an endlessly indulgent, if totally capricious, parent.[32]

At the root of this distorted version of the Christian faith lies a *reduction*. The full teaching of the New Testament and the great Tradition has been cut down to only two themes, or rather, preoccupations: *sin* (for which a wrathful God will exact just punishment) and *grace* (merited by the suffering of an innocent person and gratuitously bestowed on the elect by a sovereign God, for their salvation). This reduction, along with the ensuing distortion, has not been totally unknown in the Catholic church, especially in Jansenist circles, though it has never been typical of mainstream Catholicism. The churches of the continental Reformation, however, with their native tendency to make salvation the central theme of the gospel,[33] have been more affected by it. It became the dominant theme in the free churches of the congregational, Evangelical type, with their strong emphasis on individual, deeply emotional assurance of salvation, and through them, in the mainstream denominations of North America.

Conclusion

We have reviewed three dubious developments. It is not difficult to recognize in them three principal causes of friction between Christianity and Judaism, all of them pointed out and criticized by Levinas. The first—Christianity's status as an established religion— accounts for the fact that the Christian concept of fulfillment got misinterpreted as *displacement of Judaism*. The second—dependency as a widespread characteristic of the Christian style of believing— accounts for the prominence of the salvation theme in Christian believing, at the expense of the theme of moral responsibility for humanity and the world. The third—salvation by substitutionary Atonement—accounts for the tendency, excoriated by Levinas, to mystify suffering and thus justify it.

From the point of view of Christian, Catholic theology, and in the name of the gospel and the great Tradition of the undivided Christian Church, we have to say that on all three counts, the type of Christian faith that Levinas rejects is one that deserves to be rejected. In demanding (1) that Judaism be respected in its own integrity, (2) that faith in God be construed, not as an assurance of divine indulgence to comfort the immature, but as a divine call to disciplined maturity, and (3) that the suffering of the innocent not be mystified and thus justified, Levinas is simply asking Christians to be true to their own deepest tradition.

3. Mutuality, Eschatology, Humanism

It is time to wind up. Three points remain to be made. I wish to argue that the relationship between Jews and Christians, (and especially Catholic Christians) can be characterized by *mutuality*, by a *shared, eschatological faith-commitment*, and by a *humanism committed to a civilized world*.

To begin with, Christianity and Judaism are inseparable. It is true that the relationship is asymmetrical: Judaism came to believe in Christianity, and not the other way round. But Christianity has not supplanted Judaism, not even for Christians. First of all, Christians continue to acknowledge the same God as the Jews, and like Jews, they relate to God not in a merely philosophic manner but in an attitude of worship and obedience in which deep awe goes hand in hand with deep intimacy. Secondly and more specifically, Christians must forever bless the All-Sovereign God on account of the Christ, born from the race of Israel according to the flesh (Rom 9, 5). And this Christ is totally unintelligible apart from the context of Israel's history with its faithful God. It was Israel that was privileged "to be made God's children, to have God's glory revealed, to become partners of God in the covenants, to receive the Torah, to worship God, and to receive the divine promises" (Rom 9, 4). Thus it is only through an appreciation of Israel's faith-tradition that Christians can proclaim the risen Christ as the fulfillment of those same traditions.

By the same token, however, a true appreciation of Israel's faith-tradition must also open Christian eyes to the realization that most of God's promises remain to be fulfilled. In this way, the Scriptures of Israel as well as contemporary Judaism must be living reminders to Christians—especially to those Christians who tend to lay claim to assured salvation—that God's is the widest conceivable universe. No matter how saved I am and no matter how holy the Church, God's Kingdom has not yet come, the People of God is still being tested on its way through the desert of the Gentiles (Ez 20, 35), for God's glory has not yet been revealed to all flesh (cf. Is 40, 3-5). Judaism's sharp awareness of its *diaspora*, its *sense of the incomplete-*

ness of salvation, therefore, is its essential challenge to Christianity. That sense of incompleteness must unite Christians with Jews, just as it caused Paul to acknowledge his "sorrow and unceasing anguish" on behalf of his "relatives according to the flesh," to the point where he was still capable of imagining himself as "cut off from Christ" for their sake (Rom 9, 2-3).

Is there a challenge Christianity can offer to Judaism? The essential difference between Judaism and Christianity lies in a different interpretation of Christ's resurrection. Christians have been characterized, from the beginning, by their interpretation of Jesus' resurrection as *the dawn of the messianic age*; Jews, even those exceptional Jews that accept Jesus' resurrection, can go no further than giving Jesus a place of honor in the *preparation of the messianic age*. But even in this more limited perspective, Christians can confirm Jews in their yearning for the resurrection[34] —that is to say, for the establishment of a world of definitive justice. For Christians, that justice is a matter not only of aspiration but of a firm hope held out by God in the person of Jesus Christ risen, "the Holy and Just One" (Acts 3, 14). This hope is decisively colored by the conviction that *nothing whatever*, not even the worst disaster or injustice, can separate us from the love of God (cf. Rom 8, 39). This latter point leads to a further, more fundamental reflection.

In Christ risen, Christians believe, final justice is revealed as having a dimension that puts faith in God—the faith of Jews and Christians alike—to a final test. The definitive justice that is achieved by God comes about, not by the crushing of all injustice, but by God taking it on and absorbing and outsuffering it. That is to say, final justice will reveal a God who is the God of the just and the unjust alike (cf. Mt 5, 45). In other words, Christians believe, at the word of Jesus and on the assurances held out in the resurrection of the One unjustly crucified, that God *can* "after all be the God of those whose deeds are the most horrible expression of ungodliness."[35] Could it be that Jews can learn from the Christian conviction that God's will for universal salvation operates by *overcoming evil with good* (cf. Rom 12, 21)? After all, Christians first learned this conviction from Israel's wisdom: "If your enemy is hungry, give him bread to eat, and if he is thirsty, give him water to drink; for you will heap coals of fire on his head, and the Lord will reward you" (Prov 25, 21-22). An inner commitment to this truth can be based only on a sense of mystery— that is, on the worship of a God whose utter love is matched only by utter incomprehensibility.

On the basis of this eschatological faith-commitment common to Judaism and Christianity, therefore, both Jews and Christians can go back to the heart of their respective faiths to seek guidance for the responsible life. Both Jews and Christians are indeed committed to the betterment of humanity and the world, but *union with God*, not faith in progress is the basis for their confidence in the potential of both. There are a hundred admirable ways to become better, more just, and more humane, but the way of true justice is learned from the word of God alone. Neither Jews nor Christians are sanguine about untutored human effort; they know that humanity tends to be self-maintaining and self-righteous; we do justice with a vengeance, without compassion. Only faith in the one, true God, whose transcendence sets an ever-receding, demanding standard of moral excellence, can prevent us from settling for less than Jerusalem—the vision of peace that reveals the full glory of God. In the name of God, therefore, Jews and Christians must learn how to challenge each other to repent of the violence of their justice and refer each other back to the transcendent mystery of the God they worship so as to have their feet guided into the way of peace (cf. Lk 1, 79). An eschatological faith-commitment involves a commitment to the urgent quest for peace with justice in the world now.

Christians, meanwhile, must not formulate or commend this high purpose without serious self-examination. History is written, not by victims but by victors, and often in the interest of self-justification. Up until fairly recently, the history of the West has been the history of a triumphant Christianity, inclined to depict itself as reflecting the one true God. And often, with utter disregard of its own doctrine about the unity of the Testaments, the Christian Church has characterized the God of the Hebrew Bible as the God of wrath, vengeance, and justice, over against the God of the New Testament—the God of grace, mercy, and love. It sounded as if the words of the Lord passing before Moses in Exodus (Ex 34, 6-7) had been canceled from the Hebrew Bible as the Christians knew it. We modern Christians, therefore, would do well to remember that the God worshiped by the Jews is no less the God of love than the God who is the Father of our Lord Jesus Christ. But there is even more wisdom to be found here, as a modern Christian New Testament scholar reminds us:

> An introduction to the Jewish faith is objectively necessary to make Jesus' preaching intelligible today. It is to Judaism that we owe the faith in the One and Only God. For a long time this faith was self-evident. Today it is a minority opinion. Since it is, historically and objectively, the most important presupposition of Jesus' preaching, it must be made accessible anew today.
>
> Here the Jewish origin of this faith is helpful. Christian faith in God has often been fundamentally compromised by its entanglement with power and domination. A persecuted minority for centuries, Jews have more credibly testified that the God of the Bible is not on the side of the powerful and the dominating.[36]

Christians, therefore, would do well to remember that the Torah, for all the violence of its threats, was always ever so leniently and humanely applied. The ocean of blood that has been made to flow in the name of the God of Love calls for self-critical memory on the part of Christians, not self-comforting oblivion.[37]

Finally, given their eschatological commitment to peace rooted (to use Levinas' words) in "difficult worship," Jews and Christians can also find a common ground in the challenge of "an integral and austere humanism" redounding to "the exaltation of Man."[38] This is where, in my opinion, Judaism is most closely related to the Catholic tradition within Christianity. In the Catholic tradition, what is at the heart of the Christian faith is not the human need for salvation and its fulfillment by God's mercy, but the glorification of God, which is the source as well as the consummation of humanity and the world. In this frame of things, the world shows forth the divine glory, and humanity, made in God's image and likeness, is revealed to better advantage according as it becomes more responsible. This responsibility is a matter of high privilege and election: not every nation has been favored with such depth of knowledge of God and God's ordinances (Deut 4, 7-8. 32-40; Ps 147, 19-20), and the recognition of Jesus Christ as the Torah made flesh is a matter, not of human choosing, but of being chosen (Jn 15, 16). The responsibility is exercised by appreciatively and creatively taking up the challenge of representing God in the world, by turning it to human growth and enjoyment, and thus humanizing it, with realism ("austere") and without settling for second best ("integral"). After all, before the countenance of God we have to know our place, and our place is this world. As the psalmist puts it: "The heavens are the Lord's heavens; but the earth he has given to the children of Adam" (Ps 115, 16). In that sense, Catholics can agree with Levinas' injunction that we should "love the Torah more than God." If we wish to claim we love God, that claim will be found true only to the extent that we are found to do justice, as a matter of life and death, to the humanity and the world entrusted to us, and this not by thought and slogan but in deed and in truth (cf. 1 Jn 3, 18). If our commitment aims at anything less, our claim that we love God will be empty because merely self-serving.[39]

And so, finally, I come to the extreme of buoyancy to which I promised I would carry my theological reflections about the relationship between Jews and Christians. Could it be that the taste for humane, disciplined civilization that Catholic Christianity has in common with Judaism somehow already underlies the vigorous interest so many Jews take in being involved, in a variety of ways, in such a deeply Christian and especially Catholic venture as a Catholic university?

Notes

Notes to the Introduction

1. Cf., e. g., *Anti-Judaism in Early Christianity*, Vol. 1, *Paul and the Gospels*, edited by Peter Richardson, with David Granskou.

2. Cf. section 4 of the *Declaration on the Relationship of the Church to Non-Christian Religions* promulgated by the second Vatican Council.

3. *Ad Magnesios* 10 (*The Apostolic Fathers*, Vol. I, edited by Kirsopp Lake, pp. 206-207).

4. The Jewish-inspired universalism of the passage lies in the allusion to Isaiah 66. The variant text found in the longer recension of Ignatius' letters—a late fourth-century forgery—explicitly makes this point that Judaism is dated: "It is out of place to profess Jesus Christ with the tongue, and to have in mind Judaism, which has been brought to a close [*ton pausthenta joudaismon epi dianoias echein*]" (*The Apostolic Fathers*, edited by J. B. Lightfoot, Pt. II, 3, p. 175; italics added.)

5. *Letters of St. Bernard of Clairvaux*, translated by Bruno Scott James, p. 466.

6. Arthur A. Cohen's passionate *The Myth of the Judeo-Christian Tradition* remains a significant Jewish statement of this conviction.

7. Horror of the Holocaust can give Christians access, not only to Judaism, but also to the historical Jesus: "You indicate in your letter that my assessment of Judaism resounds with horror about the Holocaust. Of course you are right! Of course I am wearing "particular lenses," as you put it. But isn't sympathy better than aversion and hatred? Perhaps we should be arguing, not so much about our "lenses," as about what we see with their help! Through them, we may come to see something new in the historical Jesus, too!" (Gerd Theissen, *Der Schatten des Galiläers*, p. 55; cf. ET *The Shadow of the Galilean*, p. 36).

8. The person who made the identification was Barry Walfish, who was, in 1974, the assistant librarian at Regis College, then located in Willowdale, Ontario, now in Toronto.

9. The literal translation of the Yiddish title is "Yossel Rakover Speaks to God." In a letter dated June 3, 1988, Mr. Kolitz informs me that he now prefers this to the original title *Yossel Rakover's Appeal to God.*

Notes to Section One

1. For this condensed account of the last two and a half years of the Warsaw ghetto, narrated in detail in many other, more recognized publications, I have relied on the recollections, recently published in English, of a non-Jewish Polish resistance fighter who participated in the final struggle: Wladyslaw Bartoszewski, *The Warsaw Ghetto: A Christian's Testimony.*

2. *The Tiger Beneath the Skin,* pp. 81-95. In 1969, Mr. Kolitz published a much-revised, though substantially identical, version of the story in his collection *Survival for What?*, pp. 201-211. The exclusion of this later version from consideration in this volume is based, not on a judgement of its quality, but on the decision to limit the present discussion to the original version and the developments it gave rise to. The later version, incidentally, shows features that would seem to indicate that it is indebted, in places, to the anonymous Yiddish version about to be discussed.

3. *Die Goldene Kaït* 18 (1954): 102-110.

4. *'Anî Ma'mîn,* edited by Mordecai Eliab, pp. 213-218. The reference to the "will" is found on p. 7, in the table of contents.

5. The letter is found in the 1971-2 volume of the Israeli periodical *Shedemoth* (Nr. 45, pp. 91ff.). Kolitz wrote: "Dear Friends: A few months ago, my brother Haim Kolitz, who lives in Jerusalem, sent me issue no. 43 of *Shedemoth,* which contained a quotation from a story entitled *Yosl Rakover Argues with his God,* which the writer of the article uses as an authentic testament, allegedly found in the Warsaw ghetto. Now I want to draw your attention to the fact that this *Yosl Rakover* is not a will which was discovered in the ruins of the ghetto, but an original story which I wrote and published about twenty years ago in New York [...]. My attention has also been called to the fact that in a book, I believe [...], to which the author of the article in *Shedemoth* was probably referring, this story of mine was published as a will. This error has apparently been repeated again and again, as has become known to me after the fact, ever since, in 1953, a great Yiddish poet, Avram Sutzkever, was misled by a Jew from Argentina, who had read the

story in Yiddish and passed it on to Sutzkever as a "document."
Mr. Sutzkever published it as such in *Die Goldene Kait* [...]. Meanwhile
the origin of this error has become clear, but errors like these have a life
of their own. The refusal of this particular error to die, and the fact that
many persons, and capable ones to boot, like Mr. Sutzkever, who
were in the ghetto (which is not the case with me), saw *Yosl Rakover* as
something that gives an authentic expression to the spiritual turmoil
of a believing Jew in the last hours of the Warsaw ghetto—all of this is
certainly a source of satisfaction to me. But there is a further testimony here. It is the testimony of my own spiritual turmoil, which did
not subside with my giving it a fictional (and, I hope, artistic) expression; it went to the depth of the pain of a people that has the awesome
right to take God to court. [...]."

6.   An example of this is the version of the story as it appeared, "by permission of the author," in 1968, in *Out of the Whirlwind*, an anthology
edited by Albert Friedlander, pp. 390-399.

Friedlander replaces the original epigraph by the following introduction: "Zvi Kolitz, who co-produced Hochhuth's *The Deputy* in New
York, has studied the Shoah and its implications for many years. In his
quest for meaning, he came to know the story of the Rakovers, a family
of Chasidim who were wiped out by the Nazis. And he wondered:
How would a Chasid, a pious Jew of Eastern Europe filled with the
spirit of men like Levi Yitzchak of Bertichev—how would such a Jew
address himself to God at this time? There is no actual document
written by Yossel Rakover. But there was a Yossel Rakover who died
in the flames. And there is the tradition of those who trust in God
though He slay them. And Kolitz's reconstruction of the last thoughts
of a pious Jew has become a small classic which has been utilized in the
Yom Kippur liturgy of university students at Yale and elsewhere. If we
say with Zvi Kolitz that Jews did pray in this manner in those final
days, one question remains: Can we, the survivors, pray in the same
manner?"

The changes made in the text itself, by an anonymous editor, are all
minor, yet they are so numerous that patterns emerge, allowing us to
identify the editor's concerns with a fair measure of probability. (1)
Quite a few changes have been introduced in the interest of *improvement of sense*; most of these occur in the first half, and all of them are of
the "tuck pointing" variety. (2) In many places, mainly in the second
half, *emphases* are added, by means of exclamation marks and by other
means. (3) There are three instances where *changes appear to have been
introduced to prevent misinterpretation*—possibly even to counteract
negative Christian stereotypes of alleged Jewish ideas: "pious" instead of "righteous" [7], "happy and well off" instead of the blunt

"well off" [99], and "waging just battles" instead of "waging battle" [128]. (4) There would appear to be a tendency towards emphasizing the *religious* dimension in places where the original is either merely allusive or downright secular: pronouns with a divine reference are consistently capitalized, there are direct references to faith [195, 253,262,314,338,342], and in one case, the divine name is replaced by the reverential circumlocution "his maker" [329]. This feature is very obvious at the end, where efforts at improvement of sense and additional emphasis are combined with changes designed to bring out the religious dimension: "shall"—connoting obligation—instead of the self-willed "will," the added emphasis on fidelity in the teeth of divine testing, and the addition of the explicit profession of faith: *"a believer!"* [336-342]. (5) Finally, the original already excoriates those who remain passive onlookers, either because of human respect or because they are secretly happy with the effects of the injustice inflicted on the Jews [286-305]; the Friedlander text would seem to want to emphasize this theme [204-205, 252-253,303-304].

7. One is reminded of Luther's insistence that the suffering of Christ is indeed a revelation of God, but by contrast—*sub contrario.*

8. One is reminded of Dietrich Bonhoeffer's decision to take his distance, not just from the German Christians who collaborated with Hitler, whom he had opposed from the start, but also from the Confessing Church, when he noticed that the latter was interested only in its own rights, and was unwilling to stand up for the Jews. Cf., for example, my *Christ Proclaimed*, pp. 484-485.

9. Cf. Paul M. van Buren's discussion of Emil Fackenheim's three questions, in his *A Theology of the Jewish-Christian Reality*, Part 3, *Christ in Context*, pp. 71-73.

10. Quoted without specific reference in Arthur Green, *Tormented Master: A Life of Rabbi Nahman of Bratslav*, p. 148. The expression is connected with Rabbi Nahman's (1772-1810) insistence on *hitbodekut* (meditation in solitude); cf. pp. 145-148. The Yiddish version of Kolitz' story quotes the saying as *Nito ken gantsere zakh fun a tsebrokhn harts* ("Nothing more whole than a broken heart").

Notes to Section Two

1. "Une religion d'adultes," in *Difficile liberté*, pp. 24-41 (originally published in 1957).

2.   Republished in: *Difficile liberté*, pp. 189-193.

3.   In making this point, it would seem that Levinas has primarily the hasidic masters in mind.

4.   Cf. "Simone Weil contre la Bible," in *Difficile liberté*, pp. 178-188.

5.   "C'est la clarté platonicienne qui hante Simone Weil": "Simone Weil contre la Bible," in *Difficile liberté*, p. 187.

6.   Cf. the striking passage in "Simone Weil contre la Bible", *Difficile liberté*, p. 183.

7.   Cf. J.-M. Perrin et G. Thibon, *Simone Weil telle que nous l'avons connue* (ET *Simone Weil As We Knew Her*).

8.   The bibliography on Simone Weil is considerable. For a first introduction to her person and her thought, cf. E. Piccard, *Simone Weil: Essai biographique et critique suivi d'une Anthologie raisonnée des oeuvres de Simone Weil*; Simone Weil, *Waiting for God*; Id., *Gravity and Grace*; Simone Pétrement, *Simone Weil: A Life*; E. W. F. Tomlin, *Simone Weil*; John Hellman, *Simone Weil: An Introduction to her Thought*; George A. Panichas' *Simone Weil Reader*. Cf. also the *Réponses aux questions de Simone Weil*. Not surprisingly, Simone Weil has been claimed by more than one intellectual constituency, not all of them quite compatible with each other, as a quick comparison of the prefaces to the above works will show.

9.   Cf., e. g., Walter Lowrie's edition of *Fear and Trembling* and *The Sickness Unto Death*.

10.   To the extent that these comments are intended, by Levinas, as a fundamental criticism of Kierkegaard, they must be called inadequate. Kierkegaard may be largely unaware of the ethical imperative involved in faith, he knows the difference between an immature faith that is merely self-regarding and the mature faith that truly regards God: "for he who loves God without faith reflects upon himself, he who loves God believingly reflects upon God" (*Fear and Trembling* and *The Sickness Unto Death*, p. 47).

11.   Cf. Melanchthon's statement: "All the benefits of the Gospel are included in the idea of the forgiveness of sins" (Quoted by Hans Engelland in *Melanchthon on Christian Doctrine: Loci Communes 1555*, p. xl).

12. On this theme, cf. Walter Brueggemann, "The Triumphalist Tendency in Exegetical History." For a fuller treatment of the issue, with special emphasis on John Henry Newman's treatment of the issue, cf. my *God Encountered: A Contemporary Catholic Systematic Theology*, Vol. 1, *Understanding the Christian Faith*, §20.

13. Cf. the end of "Simone Weil contre la Bible," in *Difficile liberté*, p. 188.

14. The figure of Sigmund Freud, obviously, comes to mind.

15. Cf. *Letters and Papers from Prison* (many editions), the entries under June 8, July 16 (which also contains striking parallels to Levinas' rejection of faith conceived as a *salto mortale* and as a return to infancy) and August 3, 1944 (note esp. the expression: "Decisive: Church in self-defense. No risk-taking on behalf of others.").

16. "Une nouvelle version de «Jésus raconté par le Juif Errant», d'Edmond Fleg," in *Difficile liberté*, p. 140.

17. The analysis here given has some affinity with Feodor Dostoevsky's dramatic "Legend of the Grand Inquisitor," in *The Brothers Karamazov* (V, 5), which explains that the most fundamental feature of Roman Catholicism is immaturity, concretized in the belief that Christ has handed over everything to the Pope and to the hierarchy. This has deprived the faithful of direct access to Christ, and left nothing but a debased version of the Christian faith, accommodated to the needs of an irresponsible populace craving for assurance. Thus the Church of Christ is replaced by a totalitarian theocracy run by a clergy that has itself lost all faith. Ivan, the atheist who tells the story in *The Brothers Karamazov*, implicitly agrees that this is the only form of Christianity that is practical, thus making the charge against the Catholic Church even more devastating.

18. On neuroticizing influences in a culture, cf., for example, Karen Horney's chapter on "Culture and Neurosis," in *The Neurotic Personality of Our Time*, pp. 281-290.

19. In the language of Christian soteriology, what Levinas calls "substitution" is usually, and more appropriately, called "vicariousness" or "representation," and not "substitution," which has connotations of "replacement." Cf. below, pp. 76-77. Cf. also my *Christ Proclaimed*, pp. 410-417, and "Ten Questions on Christology and Soteriology," esp. pp. 276-277.

20.   Cf. "La substitution," esp. pp. 499ff..

21.   Cf. "Une religion d'adultes," In *Difficile liberté*, pp. 24-41, esp. 36-38; quotation p. 38.

22.   "Une religion d'adultes," in *Difficile liberté*, p. 37.

23.   "Bien sûr qu'il me pardonnera; c'est son métier." Quotation found in Bergen Evans' *Dictionary of Quotations*, p. 158, and identified as Heine's reply to a priest who had told him that God would forgive him his sins. Evans adds Freud's famous explanation of the saying as a classic instance of projection.

Curiously, none of the authoritative lives of Heine mention the incident; Jeffrey L. Sammons is probably on target when he writes (*Heinrich Heine: A Modern Biography*, p. 344): "Like all nineteenth-century eminences, he was ascribed last words, and, of course, in several widely different versions." In any case, the saying does fit the mood of Heine's religiosity during his last years, spent in debilitating infirmity. Hugo Bieber's *Heinrich Heine: Gespräche—Briefe, Tagebücher, Berichte seiner Zeitgenossen* does not mention the saying, but it does mention outbursts like the following: "I make no secret of my Judaism; I have not returned to it because I never left it. I let myself be baptized, but not because I hated Judaism. I have never been serious about my atheism. My former friends, the Hegelians, have proved to be louts. Human misery is too great. We *must* believe" (p. 297). Or: "Christianity, with all its forms of resignation and all its biases, is useless for the healthy. But let me assure you, it is a pretty good religion for the sick" (p. 330). And: "Just think of the pleasure of being able to recount one's sweetest sins in front of someone else, and to obtain the assurance that the good Lord rejoices more over the penitent sinner [*die büßende Sünderin—feminine!*] than over a hundred just people" (p. 404). For similar instances, cf. pp. 325, 370, 383.

24.   Cf. *The Cost of Discipleship*, esp. pp. 37-114; also cf. note 14 above.

Notes to Section Three

1.   Above, p. 2.

2.   Cf. above, p. 5.

3.   Above, p. 3.

4. On this subject, cf. my *God Encountered: A Contemporary Catholic Systematic Theology*, Vol. 1, *Understanding the Christian Faith*, §40, 3.

5. Above, p. 1.

6. *To Love the Torah More than God*, lines 158-160, p. 39; cf. also above, pp. 34, 52-53.

7. On this subject, cf. *God Encountered: A Contemporary Catholic Systematic Theology*, Vol. 1, *Understanding the Christian Faith*, §33, 2.

8. For the author of 2 Maccabees, the expectation of the resurrection to come implied that it was a sacred duty to pray for the dead, especially since they had been found guilty of sin: 2 Macc 12, 39-45.

9. The latter is a major theme in Luke's Gospel, which presents Jesus as personally explaining the Scriptures: Lk 24, 25-27. 44-45; cf. 22, 37; cf. also 2, 46-47.

10. Heb 3, 2-6 calls both Moses—the giver of the Law—and Jesus "faithful" in God's household, but casts the former in the role of the majordomo, the latter in the role of the son of the lord of the household.

11. There may be traces of wisdom-christology in Matthew, too; cf. Mt 11, 19c. For a careful (if somewhat overly "johannine" and "incarnationist") account of the origins of pre-existence christology, cf. James D. G. Dunn, *Christology in the Making*. For the prologue of John, cf. a recent paper, to be published in the *Catholic Biblical Quarterly*, by my friend and colleague Thomas H. Tobin, S.J., "The Prologue of John and Hellenistic Jewish Speculation."

12. The synoptic passion accounts reinforce this point by drawing on the *prophetic* tradition: they cast Jesus in the role of the patient servant of Is 52, 13 - 53, 12. This involves a martyrial account of Jesus' sufferings: they identify Jesus as a *witness* to God's faithfulness, and thus as God's servant. Cf. Acts 8, 32-33 for an explicit quotation.

13. Cf. *Yossel Rakover's Appeal to God*, lines 226-228; above, p. 21.

14. *To Love the Torah More than God*, lines 94-97; above, p. 38. Cf. *Yossel Rakover's Appeal to God*, lines 271-279; above p. 23. Cf. also above, pp. 27-28, 47-48.

15.   Two points, heavy with consequence, on which there is, allegedly, a discrepancy between the teaching of Jesus in the New Testament and the Jewish tradition, including the utterances of Yossel in Kolitz' story, must at least be acknowledged, even if it is impossible to treat the issues fully here.

The first point concerns the recognition of God as *the God of the just as well as the unjust.* Yossel prays: "You are not, You cannot after all be the God of those whose deeds are the most horrible expression of ungodliness" [lines 273-274]. Jesus, on the contrary, teaches his disciples to love their enemies and to pray for their persecutors, "so that you may be children of your Father in heaven, for he makes his sun rise on the wicked and on the good, and lets the rain fall on the just and the unjust" (Mt 5, 45). Here it is important to note that Yossel's sentiment should not simply be attributed to Judaism as such, since what Jesus teaches is not unknown in universalist Judaism (cf., e. g., Prov 25, 21-22), as the New Testament recognizes (Rom 12, 20).

The second point, connected with the first, concerns the issue—very complicated in the Hebrew Scriptures—of *vengeance,* so emphatically glorified by Yossel as an appropriate and religiously satisfying response to the enemies devastating the ghetto. Here again, Christians should be careful not to reject vengeance out of hand as "belonging to the Old Testament" and "un-Christian." There is no doubt that Israel is fundamentally assured that vengeance is the prerogative of God (Deut 32, 35; cf. Ps 94, 1; Is 35, 4); hence the Torah's injunction against retaliation among the children of Israel (Lev 19, 18). The historical Jesus shares that conviction. But he does extend the Torah's prohibition to the Gentiles, and he positively teaches voluntary long-suffering instead of revenge (Mt 5, 38-40). But this does not dispose, not even in the New Testament, of the whole idea of divine vengeance (Rev 6, 10; 16, 6; 19, 2); nor does it cancel the idea, so common in the Hebrew Scriptures, and so prominent in Yossel's prayer [lines 124-148], that human agents can be, *and even volunteer to be,* the instrument of the divine wrath or vengeance (Rom 13, 3-4; 1 Pet 2, 14).

All of this, of course, is made all the more pressing by the *modern* issue of the Christian attitude toward retributive justice and just warfare—*an issue which it is impossible to ignore when reflecting on the Holocaust.*

One of the principal differences between the Hebrew Scriptures and the New Testament lies in the fact that the former—at least in certain layers of its composition—envisions the situation in which the community of believers as such must take responsibility for public order and safety, whereas the latter does not. Not until the fourth century, when the safeguarding of the common good became a responsibility of Christians, and increasingly also of officers of the

Church, did the Christian community begin to develop an ethic of just punishment and just war.

These have become, in modern times, especially as a result of the unscrupulous technologizing of warfare, difficult issues, too complex to be fully treated here. In the present context, however, one remark must be made, lest some Christian readers of Kolitz' story should feel superior to Jews on inadmissible grounds. It is clear that there is a crying need in our day for an examination of the Christian conscience in matters of retributive justice and just warfare. Still, principled, universal, unconditional, non-selective opposition, on the part of Christians, to the use of all force and violence must not be allowed to claim superiority over the alleged Old-Testament ethic in these matters. This is especially the case if such an allegedly Christian ethic of non-violence is supported simply by out-of-context quotations from the New Testament. There are (at least) two reasons for this.

First, the New Testament, as pointed out, does not envision the case in which Christians must take responsibility for the public good, and hence, it cannot be quoted in direct support of ethico-political positions today. Secondly, there is the experience of those of us who came out of World War II with our lives to be reckoned with. We find it hard to call the war which put an end to aggressive National Socialism morally irresponsible, no matter how immoral some of the Allies' military decisions may in fact have been, and no matter how skeptical we must all be with regard to any use of force, given the strong human propensity to over-respond to injustice by more injustice.

But does this mean that justice must be assumed to be simply on the side of the absolutely non-violent? For all the nobility of expressed purpose, I seem to have noticed that advocacy of unconditional non-violence can have a curiously self-justifying ring about it. If this observation should be correct, it could also be pointed out that this brand of pacifism might just be an exact instance of the kind of religious and moral immaturity that Levinas denounces in Christianity. Claiming that God's saving love absolutely demands of me that I remain unrelated to any violence might in reality be an attitude of childish cowardice, by which I refuse to take responsibility in behalf of others who are suffering, simply in the interest of claiming a God who saves the saved.

On the question whether the early Christians were pacifists, cf. John Helgeland, Robert J. Daly, and J. Patout Burns, *Christians and the Military: The Early Experience*. On Dietrich Bonhoeffer's position on this issue, cf. above, note 8 to Section One, p. 88, and note 15 to Section Two, p. 90.

16. Cf. above, pp. 28-29.

17. *To Love the Torah More than God*, lines 76-78, p. 38. Cf. also p. 46.

18. Above, pp. 59-60.

19. Wilhelm Thüsing makes this important point well when he explains that Karl Rahner's designation of Jesus Christ as the "absolute bringer of salvation" tends to obscure the fact that there remains a *Verheißungsüberschuß*—a part of the promised salvation that remains to be fulfilled. Cf. Karl Rahner and Wilhelm Thüsing, *Christologie— systematisch und exegetisch*, pp. 104-107 (ET *A New Christology*, pp. 63-64).

20. This is, in fact, one of the pervasive themes of Paul's first Letter to the Corinthians.

21. For example, a careful reading of the elaborate ethical exhortation of Rom 12, 1 — 15, 13 will uncover numerous quotations from the Jewish Scriptures, especially the sapiential ones.

22. One of the pervasive themes in Paul's first Letter to the Corinthians is that freedom breaks down into components—specific attitudes and commitments, summed up under the heading of *agape*.

23. The determination to be universalist and catholic in relation to Judaism, and not sectarian and narrow, therefore, is integral to the faith of the Christian Church.

   Never, perhaps, was this demonstrated more forcefully than in the mid-second century. It took the shape of the rejection of *Marcionism*, the most widespread and successful of the second-century heresies, as well as the prototype of all subsequent forms of sectarian rigorism in the Christian Church. In his eagerness to proclaim the newness of the Christian revelation, Marcion saw the Gospel, not as the mandate for the *ongoing* fulfillment of the history of Israel and the world, but as its definitive *replacement*. In Marcion's view, Judaism was simply one religion among many, and the God of the Jews was none other than the subordinate Demiurge—the Creator-God who had made the world and who had exacted obedience to the law. The Gospel (Marcion thought that Paul had been the only one to understand it fully) had at long last proclaimed "the greatest God"—the God of Love revealed by Jesus Christ. Faced with this challenge, the Christian tradition opted for a difficult redemptive task, rather than a sectarian and self-righteous one. It resigned itself to asking and answering the many hard questions about the true meaning of the Jewish Scriptures and the religions of the world, and refused to turn itself into a completely novel creation with no real responsibilities to the world of time and place. (Cf. my *God Encountered: A Contemporary Catholic Systematic Theology*, Vol. 1, *Understanding the Christian Faith*, §40, 3, d.)

24. Cf. Glenn F. Chesnut's fine summary of the concluding paragraphs of the tenth and last book of Eusebius' Ecclesiastical History, in his *The First Christian Histories: Eusebius, Socrates, Sozomen, Theodoret, and Evagrius*, p. 118.

In the passage just preceding the one summed up by Professor Chesnut, there is a piece of extraordinary rhetoric, which shows how Eusebius views the Constantinian establishment as simply part of salvation history. He does so by tacitly casting Constantine and his son Crispus as mirror-images of God and God's Son (Gk. *pais*; this, incidentally, also intimates Eusebius' subordinationist christology): "[...] because they had as guides and comrades-in-arms *God, the sovereign King* and *the Son of God, Savior of all*, the two of them, *father and son*, [...] gain an easy victory. [...] The most great victor Constantine, excelling in every virtue connected with the service of God, together with his son, emperor most beloved by God and in all respects resembling his father, [...] established the one unified empire of the Romans as of old" (*Hist. Eccl.*, X, 9, 4. 6; *Sources chrétiennes* 55, pp. 119-120).

On Eusebius' presentation of the Emperor as the "epiphany of Christ," cf. Chesnut's illuminating chapter "Eusebius: Hellenistic Kingship and the Eschatological Constantine": *op. cit.*, pp. 133-166, esp. 153-162.

25. Cf. the dogmatic constitution on the Church (*Lumen Gentium*), sections 5-6.

26. I have endeavored to interpret these developments in my *Catholic Identity after Vatican II: Three Types of Faith in the One Church*, and in *God Encountered*, Vol. I, *Understanding the Christian Faith*, §54.

27. Cf. the Dogmatic Constitution on the Church *Lumen Gentium*, esp. nrs. 9-10, 40-41.

28. The New Testament uses several Greek prepositions translated by "for": *hyper* ("Christ died for all": 2 Cor 5, 14-15), *peri* ("he is the expiation for our sins": 1 Jn 2, 2), and *dia* ("for whom Christ died": 1 Cor 8, 11). There is another Greek preposition meaning "for": *anti*. Significantly, with the exception of the lone expression "ransom in exchange

for" (*lytron anti*: Mk 10, 45 = Mt 20, 28), the New Testament does not use *anti* in a soteriological sense.

29.   Anselm explicitly states that the dishonor offered to God by human sin calls for *either* satisfaction *or* punishment (Book I, 13), and that what actually occurred was *satisfaction not punishment*. Christ freely offered that satisfaction, in the giving up of his life in behalf of all, though he himself was innocent (Book II, 6; 11). In the interpretation rejected here, Jesus' death becomes a matter of *both* satisfaction *and* punishment—which, among other things, makes of God an angry tyrant bent on vindicating his rights.

30.   For this critical distinction, cf. Dorothee Sölle's provocative little book *Stellvertretung: Ein Kapitel Theologie nach dem "Tode Gottes"* (ET *Christ the Representative: An Essay in Theology after the "Death of God"*).

31.   Cf. my "Ten Questions on Soteriology and Christology," esp. p. 277; cf. also my *God Encountered*, Vol. 1, *Understanding the Christian Faith*, § 34, 2.

32.   Cf. above, pp. 44-45, 47.

33.   Cf. above, p. 44.

34.   Cf., for example, Pinchas Lapide, *The Resurrection of Jesus: A Jewish Perspective*.

35.   Cf. *Yossel Rakover's Appeal to God*, lines 273-274, p. 23; *To Love the Torah More than God*, lines 92-94, p. 38; cf. also p. 49.

36.   Gerd Theissen, *Der Schatten des Galiläers*, p. 55 (cf. ET *The Shadow of the Galilean*, p. 36).

37.   Cf. *Yossel Rakover's Appeal to God*, expansion at line 135, p. 19. *To Love the Torah More than God*, lines 123-129, p. 39; cf. also pp. 51-52.

38.   Cf. above, *To Love the Torah More than God*, lines 158-160, p. 40; cf. also pp. 34, 52-53.

39.   As I am putting the finishing touches on this manuscript, I am reading Nicholas Lash's fine new book *Easter in Ordinary*. In it, I am happy to find, in two illuminating chapters on Martin Buber (pp. 178-218), a number of intuitions and arguments with which the points made here are in basic harmony. They concern the dynamic relationships be-

tween Judaism and Christianity precisely as they are predicated on a far more fundamental issue: that of the correlation between humanity's relationship with the living God and its common responsibility in the real world.

Bibliography

'Anî Ma'mîn. Edited by Mordecai Eliab. Jerusalem: Mossad Harav Kook, 1965.

Anti-Judaism in Early Christianity. Vol. 1. Paul and the Gospels. Edited by Peter Richardson, with David Granskou. Studies in Christianity and Judaism, 2. Waterloo, Ontario: Wilfred Laurier University Press, 1986.

The Apostolic Fathers. Volume I. Edited by Kirsopp Lake. The Loeb Classical Library. London–New York: William Heinemann–G. P. Putnam's Sons, 1930.

The Apostolic Fathers. Pt. II/3. Edited by Joseph Barber Lightfoot. Hildesheim–New York: Georg Olms Verlag, 1973.

Bartoszewski, Wladyslaw –. The Warsaw Ghetto: A Christian's Testimony. With a Foreword by Stanislaw Lem. Boston: Beacon Press, 1987.

van Beeck, Frans Jozef –. Catholic Identity after Vatican II: Three Types of Faith in the One Church. Chicago: Loyola University Press, 1985.

—. Christ Proclaimed: Christology as Rhetoric. New York–Ramsey–Toronto: Paulist Press, 1979.

—. God Encountered: A Contemporary Catholic Systematic Theology. Vol. 1. Understanding the Christian Faith. San Francisco: Harper & Row, 1989.

—. "Ten Questions on Christology and Soteriology." Chicago Studies 25 (1986): 269-278.

[Bernard, Saint–.] Letters of St. Bernard of Clairvaux. Translated by Bruno Scott James. Chicago: Henry Regnery Company, 1953.

Bonhoeffer, Dietrich –. The Cost of Discipleship. 2nd Revised Edition. New York: Macmillan, 1963.

Brueggemann, Walter –. "The Triumphalist Tendency in Exegetical History." Journal of the American Academy of Religion 38 (1970): 367-380.

van Buren, Paul M. –. *A Theology of the Jewish-Christian Reality.* Part 3. *Christ in Context.* San Francisco: Harper & Row, 1988.

Chesnut, Glenn F. –. *The First Christian Histories: Eusebius, Socrates, Sozomen, Theodoret, and Evagrius. Théologie historique,* 46. Paris: Beauchesne, 1977.

Cohen, Arthur A. –. *The Myth of the Judeo-Christian Tradition.* New York–Evanston: Harper & Row, [1970].

Dunn, James D. G. –. *Christology in the Making.* Philadelphia: Westminster Press, 1980.

Evans, Bergen –. *Dictionary of Quotations.* New York: Delacorte Press, 1968.

Green, Arthur –. *Tormented Master: A Life of Rabbi Nahman of Bratslav.* New York: Schocken Books, 1981.

[Heine, Heinrich –.] Heinrich Heine: *Gespräche: Briefe, Tagebücher, Berichte seiner Zeitgenossen.* Edited by Hugo Bieber. Berlin: Welt-Verlag, 1926.

Helgeland, John –, Daly, Robert J. –, and Burns, J. Patout –. *Christians and the Military: The Early Experience.* Philadelphia: Fortress Press, 1985.

Hellman, John –. *Simone Weil: An Introduction to her Thought.* Philadelphia: Fortress Press, 1984.

Horney, Karen –. *The Neurotic Personality of Our Time.* New York: W.W. Norton, 1937.

Kierkegaard, Søren –. *Fear and Trembling* and *The Sickness Unto Death.* Translation, Introduction, and Notes by Walter Lowrie. Princeton: Princeton University Press, 1954.

Kolitz, Zvi –. *The Tiger Beneath the Skin: Stories and Parables of the Years of Death.* New York: Creative Age Press, 1947.

—. *Survival for What?* New York: Philosophical Library, 1969.

Lapide, Pinchas –. *The Resurrection of Jesus: A Jewish Perspective.* Minneapolis: Augsburg, 1983.

Lash, Nicholas –. *Easter in Ordinary: Reflections on Human Experience and the Knowledge of God.* Charlottesville: The University Press of Virginia, 1988.

Levinas, –. *Difficile liberté: Essais sur le judaïsme*. 3rd Edition. Paris: Albin Michel, 1976.

—. "La substitution." *Revue philosophique de Louvain* 66 (1968): 487-508.

[Melanchthon, Philipp.] *Melanchthon on Christian Doctrine: Loci Communes 1555*. Translated and edited by Clyde L. Manschrek, Introduction by Hans Engelland. New York: Oxford University Press, 1965.

Out of the Whirlwind: A Reader in Holocaust Literature. Edited by Albert Friedlander. New York: Union of American Hebrew Congregations, 1968.

Perrin, J.-M. – and Thibon, G. –. *Simone Weil telle que nous l'avons connue*. Paris: La Colombe, 1952. 2nd Edition. [Paris]: Fayard, 1967. (ET *Simone Weil As We Knew Her*. London: Routledge & Kegan Paul, 1953.)

Pétrement, Simone –. *Simone Weil: A Life*. Translated by Raymond Rosenthal. New York: Pantheon Books, 1976.

Piccard, E. –. *Simone Weil: Essai biographique et critique suivi d'une Anthologie raisonnée des oeuvres de Simone Weil*. Paris: Presses Universitaires de France, 1960.

Rahner, Karl – and Thüsing, Wilhelm –. *Christologie–systematisch und exegetisch*. Quaestiones disputatae, 55. Freiburg–Basel–Wien: Herder, 1972. (ET *A New Christology*. Translated by David Smith and Verdant Green. New York: Seabury, 1980.)

Réponses aux questions de Simone Weil. Contributions by J.-M. Perrin, J. Daniélou, C. Durand, J. Kaelin, L. Lochet, B. Hussar, J.-M. Emmanuelle. Paris: Aubier, Editions Montaigne, 1964.

Sammons, Jeffrey L. –. *Heinrich Heine: A Modern Biography*. Princeton: Princeton University Press, 1979.

Sölle, Dorothee –. *Stellvertretung: Ein Kapitel Theologie nach dem "Tode Gottes"*. 5th Edition. Stuttgart–Berlin: Kreuz-Verlag, 1968. (ET *Christ the Representative: An Essay in Theology after the "Death of God"*. Philadelphia: Fortress Press, 1967.)

Theissen, Gerd –. *Der Schatten des Galiläers: Historische Jesusforschung in erzählender Form*. Fifth Impression. München: Chr. Kaiser, 1988. (ET *The Shadow of the Galilean: The Quest of the Historical Jesus in Narrative Form*. Translated by John Bowden. Philadelphia: Fortress Press, 1987.)

Tobin, Thomas H. –. "The Prologue of John and Hellenistic Jewish Speculation." Unpublished paper.

Tomlin, E. W. F. –. *Simone Weil. Studies in Modern European Literature and Thought.* New Haven: Yale University Press, 1954.

Weil, Simone –. *Waiting for God.* Translated by Emma Craufurd. Introduction by Leslie A. Fiedler. New York: G. P. Putnam's Sons, 1951.

—. *Gravity and Grace.* Introduction by Gustave Thibon. Translated by Arthur Wills. New York: G. P. Putnam's Sons, 1952.

The Simone Weil Reader. Edited by George A. Panichas. New York: David McKay Company, 1977.

Index of Biblical References

Index of Proper Names